AF417366

TO MYSELF

A NEW TRANSLATION OF MEDITATIONS

MARCUS AURELIUS

Translated by
JAMES G. YORKE

Cover by: Filibooks Covers

Published by: Filibooks Classics

Filibooks ApS

info@filibooks.com

CVR: 37100161

©Filibooks 2024

Paperback ISBN: 978-87-94559-11-9
Ebook ISBN: 978-87-94559-12-6

CONTENTS

FOREWORD

In presenting this translation of Marcus Aurelius's private reflections, my ambition extends beyond the act of rendering ancient Greek into modern English. This work is also an exploration, a deep dive into the psyche of one of history's most complex and revered figures. Marcus Aurelius, a sovereign of immense influence, sought solace and wisdom not in the trappings of his external environment but within the confines of his own mind. These writings, intended for his eyes alone, serve as a powerful reminder of the timeless quest for personal virtue and understanding.

My approach in translating these reflections was governed by a dual imperative: to remain faithful to the original text's integrity and to ensure its relevance to today's readers. It is a delicate balance, aiming to bridge the chasm of millennia, bringing the emperor's introspective journey into the contemporary sphere. The enduring wisdom of Aurelius, his reflections on life, the cosmos, and our place within it, speaks to the core of what it means to be human, transcending the bounds of time and culture.

Aurelius's private musings reveal a man wrestling with the

questions that touch upon the essence of existence. Here, amidst the weight of empire, he contemplates reason, discipline, and the duty we owe to ourselves, and to the broader tapestry of society. His reflections offer a beacon for navigating the complexities of modern life, grounding us in principles that advocate for ethical conduct, mindfulness, and a compassionate regard for the collective well-being of humanity.

In undertaking this translation, I have sought to open a dialogue between Marcus Aurelius and the contemporary reader, fostering a connection that illuminates the shared path of human endeavor. His pursuit of philosophical truth and moral clarity provides a compass for those of us navigating the uncertainties of the 21st century, offering solace and a measure of guidance in our search for meaning.

This book, then, is an invitation: to engage with the thoughts of a man who, though separated from us by millennia, shares our deepest concerns and aspirations. It is my hope that within these pages, readers will discover a source of inspiration and reflection, a narrative that resonates with their own journey towards understanding and virtue. Marcus Aurelius, with his profound insights into the human condition, offers not just lessons from the past but a vision for a life lived with purpose and dignity in the present.

BOOK 1

1. FROM MY GRANDFATHER VERUS, I LEARNED KINDNESS AND EVEN-temperedness.

2. From the reputation and memory of my father, I learned modesty and courage.

3. My mother taught me piety and generosity; to avoid not only evil actions but even evil thoughts; and to lead a simple life, far from the extravagance of the wealthy.

4. My great-grandfather taught me to avoid public schools in favor of private tutors at home, emphasizing that one should not hesitate to spend on quality education.

5. My tutor instilled in me the importance of not favoring any chariot racing teams or gladiators; to embrace hardship and

desire little; to be industrious, mind my own affairs, and avoid gossip and meddling in others' business.

6. From Diognetus, I learned to avoid petty concerns; to dismiss the claims of miracle-workers and sorcerers; to have no interest in quail fighting; to value free speech; to embrace philosophy; to have attended lectures by Bacchius, Tandasis, and Marcianus; to have engaged in writing dialogues in my youth; and to aspire to the simplicity of the Greek discipline.

7. Rusticus taught me the importance of moral self-improvement; to avoid sophistry, speculative writing, and pretentiousness; to eschew rhetoric, poetry, and eloquence; to practice simplicity in my correspondence, as demonstrated by his own letter to my mother from Sinuessa; to be quick to forgive and reconcile with those who have wronged me, as long as they show a willingness to make amends; to read thoroughly and seek deep understanding; to be cautious in agreement; and to familiarize myself with the works of Epictetus from his personal collection.

8. Apollonius exemplified the freedom of will and unwavering resolve; to focus solely on reason; to maintain consistency in the face of pain, loss, or illness; to observe a living example of someone who is both firm and flexible; to be patient in teaching; to witness someone who regarded his ability to explain philosophical concepts as his least significant quality; and to learn how to accept kindness from friends without compromising my dignity or seeming ungrateful.

.   .   .

9. Sextus embodied kindness; he demonstrated how to lead a family with authority and live in harmony with nature; to balance seriousness and approachability; to care for friends' needs; to be patient with those lacking knowledge or who judge hastily; to be adaptable, making my company more desirable than flattery, while still commanding respect; to explore and organize life's essential principles methodically; to never display anger or any passion, maintaining a calm demeanor while being genuinely affectionate; to offer praise quietly and possess extensive knowledge without showing off.

10. From the grammarian Alexander, I learned the importance of being tactful and gently correcting those who use incorrect grammar or inelegant language—not with harsh rebukes, but by subtly offering the correct expression as if in agreement or confirmation, focusing on the topic rather than the words, or through some other polite suggestion.

11. From Fronto, I understood the deceptive nature of tyranny—its envy, duplicity, and hypocrisy—and how, more often than not, those among us hailed as "patricians" are found wanting in genuine affection.

12. From the Platonic philosopher Alexander, I learned to avoid telling others too frequently or unnecessarily, whether in person or in writing, "I am too busy," and not to constantly excuse myself from obligations to my peers by blaming external circumstances.

. . .

13. From Catulus, I learned not to dismiss a friend's complaint, even if it seems unreasonable, but to attempt to restore our previous closeness; to speak respectfully of teachers, as he did of Domitius and Athenodotus; and to genuinely care for children.

14. From my brother[1] Severus, I learned the value of family love, honesty, and justice; and through him, I was introduced to Thrasea, Helvidius, Cato, Dion, and Brutus, and envisioned a republic characterized by equal rights and freedom of speech, and a monarchy that values its subjects' liberty above all.

From him, I also learned the importance of being consistent and dedicated in valuing philosophy; to be kind, generous, hopeful, and to trust in the affection of friends; to be open with those he corrected; and to be so transparent that his friends never had to guess his desires.

15. From Maximus, I learned self-control and to remain unswayed by passions; to be cheerful in all situations, even during illness; to perfectly balance gentleness, dignity, and calm determination when pursuing goals. Everyone trusted that his words matched his thoughts and his actions were just. He was steadfast, never daunted, rushed, hesitant, confused, dejected, or pretentious; never angry or suspicious.

He was kind, forgiving, honest, and exuded a sense of innate integrity rather than mere pretense. No one felt neglected or dared to consider themselves his superior. He possessed a gracious sense of humor.

16. From my father[2], I learned to maintain an even temper, to stick to well-considered judgments; to be indifferent to superfi-

cial honors; to work diligently and persistently; to be open to listening to anyone who had ideas for the common good; to give everyone their due without bias; and to know when to apply vigor and when to show mercy.

I learned to control youthful impulses; to share goals with friends without insisting they accompany me on every outing, always finding him consistent upon their return; to be thorough and persistent in discussions, not to give up after forming initial impressions; to value friends without becoming overly attached; to be self-sufficient and cheerful in any situation.

I learned to plan even for the smallest details of life without making a fuss; to not tolerate flattery or commotion around him; to always prioritize the empire's needs, to be economical in spending, and to remain unfazed by criticism on such matters. He was neither superstitious towards the gods nor did he seek to flatter or stir up the public, but remained sober, steady, refined, and conservative.

When fortune allowed for life's luxuries, he enjoyed them without pretense—content in their presence and untroubled in their absence. No one could accuse him of being a sophist, sycophant, or pedant; rather, he was seen as experienced, integral, and capable of leading both himself and others.

He respected true philosophers without dismissing others or being overly influenced by them. He was friendly and charming in moderation. He took reasonable care of his health—neither indulging nor neglecting his body, but through his own efforts requiring little medical help.

Above all, he willingly allowed those skilled in oratory, law, customs, or any field to excel, supporting them without envy. Though he adhered to traditional ways, he did not make a display of it.

He was neither restless nor inconsistent, content with

familiar places and activities. After experiencing headaches, he quickly returned to his duties. He kept few secrets, and those only concerning state affairs. He was careful and moderate in his religious practices, public works, and gifts—focusing on the action, not the acclaim.

He bathed at appropriate times, avoided excessive construction, shunned extravagant foods, and showed no interest in fancy clothing or personal adornment. His cloak was simple, his tunic plain, his footwear basic—all reflecting his modest lifestyle.

He was neither harsh, stubborn, nor impulsive—his approach was always reasoned, calm, methodical, energetic, and consistent. The saying about Socrates fits well: he could either abstain from or enjoy those things that most find difficult to resist or indulge in excessively.

To possess strength and steadiness in both regards—that is the hallmark of a truly great man, unconquerable in spirit, as seen in Maximus' illness.

17. I have been blessed by the gods with wonderful grandfathers, parents, a sister, teachers, colleagues, relatives, and friends—nearly without exception. And I managed to avoid falling into misconduct with any of them, despite having a nature that might have led me astray under different circumstances. Thankfully, the gods never put me in such a position.

I am grateful that I was not overly influenced by my grandfather's concubine, that I maintained my innocence, and did not rush into manhood, but rather, postponed it.

I was fortunate to serve under a ruler and father who dismantled my arrogance, teaching me that one can live in a palace without the need for bodyguards, extravagant clothes, torches, statues, and other such displays of wealth; showing me it's possible to live modestly without compromising on the responsibilities one has to the community.

I had a brother whose character inspired me to better myself and who also provided me with joy through his respect and love. My children were neither unintelligent nor physically impaired. I am thankful that I did not advance further in rhetoric, poetry, and other interests, which might have consumed me had I excelled in them.

I did not delay in showing kindness to my foster parents as soon as they needed it, rather than procrastinating. I am grateful for having known Apollonius, Rusticus, Maximus.

I frequently reflected on what a natural life entails, and thanks to the gods' blessings, help, and inspiration, nothing stopped me from living in accordance with nature—though I still fall short due to my own faults, not paying enough heed to the gods' guidance.

My body has endured through this lifestyle. I resisted temptations with Benedicta and Theodotus, and even when I did succumb to love, I was able to move past it. Despite my frequent anger towards Rusticus, I never acted in a way that I would later regret.

Although my mother passed away young, she spent her final years with me. Whenever I wished to help someone in need, I was never told I didn't have the means to do so; and I never found myself in need of receiving help from others.

I am blessed with a wife who is kind, loving, and sincere. We were able to find excellent tutors for our children.

I discovered remedies through dreams, notably for preventing spitting blood and dizziness, in Caieta—as if consulting an oracle. When I turned to philosophy, I was fortunate not to fall under the influence of a sophist, nor did I waste my time on endless texts, syllogisms, or the study of celestial bodies. All these blessings I attribute to the gods and fortune.

Written among the Quadi on the banks of the Granua.

BOOK 2

1. Each morning, remind yourself: Today, I will meet people who are intrusive, ungrateful, aggressive, deceitful, jealous, and antisocial. These traits stem from their ignorance of what is truly good or evil. But I, who have recognized the beauty of goodness and the ugliness of evil, and understand that the nature of those who do wrong is similar to mine—not by blood, but through a shared rationality and a spark of the divine— cannot be harmed by them. No one can make me partake in ugliness, nor can I feel anger or hatred towards my fellow humans. We are meant to cooperate like the parts of a body— the feet, hands, eyelids, or the rows of teeth. Working against one another goes against our nature; anger and estrangement are forms of resistance.

2. Reflect on your nature: it consists of body, breath, and the governing mind. Disregard the body—it's merely flesh, bones, and a complex of nerves, veins, and arteries. Breath is nothing more than air, constantly inhaled and exhaled. The essential part is the governing mind. Consider this: You are of advanced

age; do not let yourself be enslaved by base impulses, nor be discontent with your current state or fearful of the future.

3. The actions of the gods are filled with foresight. The workings of fate align with nature and the intricate design orchestrated by providence. Everything originates from this; moreover, there's a necessity and advantage for the universe, of which you are a component. For every part of nature, what the whole's nature brings is beneficial, as is anything that sustains this nature. The universe thrives on the transformation of elements and their compounds. Let these truths suffice; let them be your firm beliefs. Abandon your craving for more knowledge, so you may not pass away in frustration but in sincere gratitude and appreciation for the gods.

4. Reflect on how long you've procrastinated, and how the gods have generously granted you extensions that you haven't utilized. It's crucial to recognize the universe you belong to, the source of your life, and that your time is limited. If you don't use it to dispel the fog from your mind, it—and you—will vanish, never to return.

5. With each hour, focus on performing your tasks with utmost integrity, compassion, autonomy, and fairness, setting aside all other concerns. This is achievable if you approach each task as if it were your last, avoiding carelessness, resistance to logic, pretense, self-indulgence, and dissatisfaction with your fate. Grasp these few principles, and you can lead a life of ease and piety; the gods will ask nothing more from someone who lives by these guidelines.

. . .

6. Continue to disgrace yourself, O soul; your time to redeem yourself is running short. Each of us is granted only one life, and yours is nearly over, yet you neglect to honor yourself, choosing instead to entrust your well-being to others.

7. Are you overwhelmed by external distractions? Then dedicate time to learn something valuable and stop your aimless wandering. But be wary of another kind of turmoil. Those who are tired of life, lacking a purpose to guide their every impulse and thought, will still act without direction.

8. It's uncommon to find someone unhappy because they neglected to consider another's thoughts. However, those who ignore the workings of their own souls are bound to be unhappy.

9. Always remember these truths: the nature of the universe, your own nature, how you relate to the universe, what part you play in it; and remember that no one can prevent you from acting and speaking in harmony with your true nature.

10. Theophrastus, comparing the nature of bad acts, asserts that actions driven by desire are worse than those driven by anger. An angry person appears to reject reason with distress and an involuntary tension. However, a person acting on desire, overwhelmed by pleasure, seems more indulgent and weaker in their faults. Philosophically, he concluded that a sin committed

for pleasure is more reprehensible than one committed in pain. The latter is more like someone wronged and driven to anger by suffering; the former willingly engages in wrongdoing, propelled by desire.

11. Approach every deed, word, and thought as if it could be your last. Departing from the company of men is not to be feared if gods exist, for they would not subject you to harm. If they do not exist or are indifferent to human affairs, why should I wish to live in a world devoid of divine presence or providence?

But they do exist and care about human affairs, equipping us with everything necessary to avoid true misfortunes. And for anything potentially harmful, they've ensured we have the means to avoid it. How can something that doesn't make a person worse, make their life worse?

It's inconceivable that the universe, through ignorance or inability, has failed to address these issues. It's equally implausible that it has erred so greatly, due to a lack of power or skill, that good and evil befall both the good and the bad indiscriminately.

Death and life, honor and disgrace, pain and pleasure, affect both the virtuous and the wicked alike, being neither noble nor base in themselves. Therefore, they are neither good nor evil.

12. Everything quickly fades away—the physical forms dissolve into the universe, and their memories into the depths of time. This is true for all things perceived through the senses, especially those that lure us with pleasure, scare us with pain, or are flaunted by vanity. They are cheap, contemptible, sordid, fleeting, and lifeless—this is what our intellect recognizes. What are these people, whose opinions and praises confer fame? What is

death, and the realization that, when viewed objectively and its impressions analyzed, it is nothing more than a natural process? And if anyone fears a natural process, they are no more than a child. Death is not only natural but also beneficial. How one connects with the divine, through which part of themselves, and the condition of that part during the connection.

13. There is nothing more pitiable than a person who endlessly circles, "digging into the things beneath the earth," as the saying goes, and guessing at the thoughts of their neighbors, without realizing that it is enough to focus on the divinity within oneself and to serve it faithfully. Serving it means keeping it free from passion, foolishness, and dissatisfaction with what comes from both gods and people. The gifts from the gods are to be revered for their excellence, and those from people are to be cherished due to kinship. And sometimes, they are pitiable, due to a lack of understanding of what is good and bad—this ignorance is as crippling as being unable to distinguish white from black.

14. Even if you were to live three thousand or thirty thousand years, always remember that one can only lose the life they are living, and live only the life they are losing. The longest and shortest lives amount to the same, for the present moment is the same for everyone, and what passes is the same for all. What seems lost is but a moment. For one cannot lose either the past or the future—how can one be deprived of what they do not possess?

Keep these two thoughts in mind: first, everything has been the same since time immemorial, going in cycles, and it matters not whether one sees the same things for a hundred, two hundred, or an infinite number of years. Second, both those who live the longest and those who will die soonest lose the same thing. For the present moment is all anyone truly has, and it's all they can lose.

15. Everything is a matter of opinion. The sayings attributed to Monimus the Cynic are evident, and the practicality of those sayings is also clear, provided one grasps the essence of their truth.

16. A person's soul inflicts harm upon itself, first and foremost, when it becomes, so to speak, a festering sore and a tumor on the universe. To resent anything that happens is to rebel against nature, which encompasses the essence of all other things. Second, it harms itself when it distances from or seeks to harm another, as those consumed by anger do. Third, when it is over-whelmed by either pleasure or pain. Fourth, when it disguises its true self with insincerity or falsehoods in words or deeds. Fifth, when it fails to align its actions or desires with a purpose, acting aimlessly and without consideration, when even the smallest actions should be undertaken with the end in mind. And for rational beings, the end is to follow the reasoning and laws of the most esteemed city and governance.

17. Human life is fleeting, its essence constantly changing, its senses limited, and the body's composition easily deteriorated. The soul is like a vortex, fortune unpredictable, and fame fleet-ing. In essence, all physical aspects are transient as a river, and what pertains to the soul is akin to dreams and mist. Life is a battle and a journey in unfamiliar territory, with posthumous recognition fading into obscurity.

What, then, can lead us? Only philosophy. This involves maintaining the divine within us intact from harm, transcending both pleasure and pain, acting deliberately, truthfully, and without pretense, independent of others' actions or inactions. Moreover, it means embracing all occurrences and destinies as emanating from the same source we originated from. Most importantly, it entails facing death with optimism, viewing it merely as the recombination of elements that constitute all living beings. If the perpetual transformation of elements is natural, why view the transformation and dissolution of everything with apprehension? For this aligns with nature, and nothing natural can be bad.

Written in Carnuntum.

BOOK 3

1. WE MUST REALIZE NOT ONLY THAT OUR LIFE DIMINISHES DAILY, leaving us with less of it, but also that even if life extends, it's not guaranteed our minds will retain their capacity to grasp concepts or engage in deep reflection on the divine and human realms. Should one's mental faculties begin to wane, the basic functions like breathing, eating, and imagining may persist, but the ability to utilize oneself, to diligently fulfill one's responsibilities, to scrutinize what is before us, to ponder if it's time to depart from life, and other such faculties demanding a sharp intellect, will fade sooner. Therefore, we must hasten not just because death approaches with each day, but also because our grasp and comprehension of life diminish before death.

2. We should also note that even the unintended results of natural processes possess a certain allure. For instance, when bread bakes and cracks open, these fissures, albeit unintended by the baker, stir a unique hunger for it.

Similarly, figs split open when at their ripest, and olives nearing decay exhibit a peculiar beauty. The bowed heads of wheat, the wrinkled snarl of a lion, the foam at a boar's mouth, among many others, might not seem attractive in isolation but, as outcomes of natural processes, they enhance their beauty and captivate.

Thus, for someone deeply attuned to nature and its mechanisms, nearly everything that naturally ensues brings some joy. Such an individual will find as much pleasure in observing the bared teeth of wild animals as in artistic representations of them. With pure appreciation, they will see beauty in the elderly and the allure in youth. These sights won't charm everyone, only those who have truly immersed themselves in nature and its phenomena.

3. Hippocrates, after curing numerous ailments, eventually succumbed to his own illness and passed away. The Chaldeans, known for predicting the demise of many, were themselves not spared by fate. Alexander, Pompey, and Julius Caesar—figures renowned for repeatedly decimating entire cities and slaughtering countless soldiers—ultimately met their own end.

Heraclitus, who extensively theorized about the universe's fiery destruction, met a grim fate, dying swollen from water retention, his body covered in cow dung. Democritus was consumed by lice, and ironically, lice also claimed the life of Socrates. What does this all mean? You boarded the ship, set sail, and now you've arrived at the harbor—it's time to disembark. If there's another life awaiting, rest assured the gods have filled it with purpose; but if it leads to oblivion, you will be freed from enduring both hardships and joys, no longer shackled to a body far inferior to what it houses—the mind and spirit, as opposed to mere dirt and decay.

· · ·

4. Don't waste the time you have left preoccupied with the lives of others—unless your thoughts contribute to the greater good. Otherwise, you're merely stealing precious moments from your own meaningful pursuits. I'm referring to obsessing over someone's actions, motives, their words, thoughts, or plans, and all other distractions that divert you from focusing on your own moral compass.

Certainly, aimless wandering of the mind must be curbed, but even more so, the intrusive and harmful thoughts. Train yourself to harbor only those thoughts you wouldn't hesitate to share if asked on the spot, "What's on your mind?" Your response should clearly reflect a person of simplicity and goodwill, someone who rejects thoughts of hedonism or self-indulgence, who is free from strife, malice, or distrust, or anything else you'd be embarrassed to admit you're pondering.

Such an individual, by not delaying the pursuit of life's ultimate goal, becomes a divine servant, attending to the inner guide that keeps one pure from pleasures, resilient to pain, immune to insult, and untainted by disgrace. This person is engaged in the highest contest: to remain unshaken by passion, deeply rooted in fairness, and fully committed to accepting whatever fate delivers, rarely—if ever—dwelling on the potential words or actions of others, unless it serves a significant communal purpose. His focus is solely on his own deeds and the universal order's ceaseless unfolding, finding beauty in the former and goodness in the latter, as each contributes to and benefits from the whole.

He also remembers that all rational beings are related, and while it's natural to care for everyone, one shouldn't seek approval from all, just from those who live in harmony with nature. As for the rest—their behavior in private and public, by night and by day, and the company they keep—he remains aware but unswayed by their opinions, for they cannot even satisfy themselves.

5. Act without reluctance, selfishness, carelessness, or mixed motives. Avoid pretense and verbosity. Do not meddle unnecessarily in the affairs of others. Let the divine within guide you, embodying the spirit of a mature, dedicated citizen, a Roman, a leader—someone who has accepted their role in life, prepared to leave without the need for promises or witnesses. Be cheerful, self-sufficient, not relying on others for your peace. Stand firm on your own, not propped up by others.

6. If you find anything in life more valuable than justice, truth, self-control, bravery—essentially, your own peace of mind in acting rationally and accepting your life's circumstances without choice—if you discover something superior, embrace it wholeheartedly and enjoy the best you've found.

However, if nothing surpasses the inner divinity guiding you, controlling your desires, scrutinizing every impression, and, as Socrates put it, free from sensory illusions, devoted to the divine and humanity—if you realize everything else is lesser, do not be swayed. If you waver, you'll struggle to prioritize your true good without distraction.

It's incorrect for external accolades, power, or pleasure to rival what is rationally and ethically right. These may seem appealing temporarily but can overwhelm and mislead you. Choose what is genuinely better, simply and with conviction. "But the useful is better," you might argue. If it benefits you as a rational being, keep it; if only as a creature of instinct, acknowledge it, and stand by your decision without pride. Ensure your judgment is sound.

·   ·   ·

7. Never consider beneficial anything that forces you to break a promise, compromise your dignity, harbor hatred, suspicion, deceit, or covet what must be hidden behind walls and curtains. One who values their intellect and its excellence above all does not play the victim, does not despair, and neither seeks solitude nor crowds; most importantly, lives indifferent to death. Whether his time in the body is long or short is of no concern. Even facing death, he departs as if undertaking any dignified, orderly task, ensuring throughout life that his thoughts never stray from what befits a rational being and a societal member.

8. In the mind of someone who is disciplined and cleansed, you won't find anything decaying, impure, or rotting. Their life isn't prematurely cut short by fate, like an actor who leaves the stage before the play is finished. Their character lacks servility, pretense, dependency, detachment, accountability, or self-centeredness.

9. Value your ability to judge wisely. Everything hinges on this, ensuring your mind no longer harbors any beliefs that clash with nature and the essence of a rational being. This guarantees immunity from rash judgments, a connection with humanity, and harmony with the divine.

10. Let go of everything else and cling to these few truths. Remember, we only live in the present moment, which is fleeting. The past is gone, and the future is uncertain. Our lives are short, our place on Earth is tiny, and even the longest-lasting fame after death is brief—relying on a chain of forgetful people

who will soon perish, unaware even of themselves, much less someone long deceased.

11. In addition to the principles already mentioned, always make it a point to clearly identify the object of your perception, seeing it plainly, in its entirety, and on its own; name it accurately and consider the elements it's made of and into which it will dissolve.

Nothing fosters a grand mindset like the ability to scrutinize and truthfully assess everything life presents, always considering how each thing is utilized in the grand scheme, its significance for the universe and for humans as citizens of the supreme city[1], of which all other cities are mere households. What is its nature and composition? How long is it meant to last, which now leaves an impression on me? What virtues does it call for from me—gentleness, bravery, honesty, loyalty, simplicity, independence, or others?

On each occasion, one should think: "This is from the divine"; "This arises from the fabric of fate, the play of chance, or similar forces"; "This comes from a family member, a friend, a colleague, who may not understand what is natural for them—but I do, so I treat them with kindness and fairness, as our common nature dictates." Yet, in matters of lesser importance, I strive to assess their true value.

12. If you approach your current task with logical thinking, dedication, vigor, and kindness—if you keep your soul clean as though you might have to give it back at any moment; if you adhere to this, fearing nothing, desiring nothing, but satisfied with your present actions in line with nature and with utmost

honesty in every word and deed, then you will live joyfully. And no one can interfere with that.

13. Just like doctors keep their instruments and scalpels at the ready for emergencies, you should have your principles prepared to understand both divine and human matters, and to approach even the smallest tasks mindful of their interconnection. Without considering the divine, you cannot excel in human affairs, and vice versa.

14. Stop wandering. You will no longer leaf through your notes, nor the histories of ancient Romans and Greeks, nor the excerpts from their writings you saved for your old age. Hurry towards the end, abandon empty hopes, and help yourself—if you care about your well-being—while there's still time.

15. Many fail to grasp the full implications of stealing, sowing, buying, being at peace, and recognizing what needs to be done —a vision not of the eyes, but of a different kind.

16. Body, soul, mind: sensations belong to the body, impulses to the soul, and principles to the mind. Being influenced by appearances is common even among animals; being driven by impulses is shared by wild beasts, the effeminate, and tyrants like Phalaris or Nero; having the mind guide us towards what seems right is possible even for atheists, traitors, and those who act in secrecy.

What sets a good person apart is their ability to accept and cherish what fate brings; not to defile the divinity within or disturb it with a multitude of impressions, but to preserve it with grace, following it as a god, speaking only truth, and acting justly. Even if others doubt his simple, modest, and content life, he remains unangered and undeterred from the path leading to life's end, where one must arrive pure, calm, willingly, and fully at peace with his fate.

BOOK 4

1. When in its natural state, the ruling power within adapts to external circumstances, not fixating on any specific outcome but keeping its desires and aversions flexible. If it encounters something favorable, it welcomes and optimizes it, much like a fire intensifies when fed more fuel, unlike a small lamp that would be extinguished.

2. Let every action be purposeful and in line with the highest standards of excellence.

3. People seek retreats in the countryside, by the sea, or in the mountains, and you too yearn for such escapes. Yet the greatest retreat is into your own soul, where you find peace and freedom unmatched elsewhere, especially when it harbors thoughts that bring immediate tranquility. Make it a habit to retreat within, refreshing yourself with principles that are concise and essential, enough to purify the soul and relieve you from dissatisfaction with external things.

Are you discontented with human flaws? Remember that humans are rational beings meant to coexist, that tolerance is part of fairness, and that errors are made unintentionally. Reflect on the countless who have perished in conflict, and find peace. If dissatisfied with your lot in the universe, consider whether it operates by providence or chance, and find peace in the realization of a greater order. If bodily concerns weigh on you, remember that the mind, once it recognizes its own strength, is untouched by physical sensations. And if the pursuit of fame troubles you, realize how quickly it fades, the vastness of time that renders it insignificant, and the fickle nature of those who bestow it.

Ultimately, retreat into your own domain without distress or strain, embracing freedom and a broad perspective—as a human, a citizen, a mortal. Among the immediate resources at your disposal, remember two things: external events do not disturb the soul, only our reactions to them do; and all you see will soon change, a truth you've witnessed time and again. The universe is in constant flux; life is shaped by our perceptions.

4. If our intellect is shared, then the logic that makes us rational beings is also shared. Consequently, the reasoning that guides what we should or should not do is common among us. If this is the case, then the law is a shared concept. This implies that we are fellow citizens, members of a political community. It follows that the universe is akin to a city. After all, what other political community can claim the entire human race as its members? From this universal city, we derive our intellectual, rational, and legal faculties. Just as my physical components are derived from various elements—my solid parts from earth, my fluids from water, my breath from air, and my warmth from fire (since nothing can emerge from nothing, nor can it vanish into noth-

ingness)—so too does our intellectual part originate from a source.

5. Death is akin to birth, a natural mystery—a blending and then a separation of the same elements. It is not something to be embarrassed about, as it does not contradict the nature of a rational being or the logic of our existence.

6. Such events are inevitable, stemming from specific causes. Wishing them away is as futile as wishing a fig tree not to produce sap. Bear in mind that in a relatively short time, both you and I will have passed away, and soon after, even our names will be forgotten.

7. Eliminate the judgment, and the idea "I have been harmed" disappears. Remove the idea, and the harm itself vanishes.

8. What does not degrade a person does not degrade his life, nor does it cause him harm, whether externally or internally.

9. The essence of what is beneficial was compelled to act in this manner.

10. "EVERYTHING THAT HAPPENS, HAPPENS JUSTLY." This becomes apparent upon careful observation. I'm not referring to simple causality, but to a deeper sense of justice, as if distributed by someone who allocates based on merit. Continue observing as

you have started, and align your actions with this principle, with the aim of being virtuous—as the true definition of a good person demands. Maintain this perspective in all your actions.

11. Do not adopt the views of those who insult you, or what they wish you to believe. Instead, see things as they truly are.

12. Keep these two guidelines at the ready: first, act only on the advice of your innermost reasoning, the part of you that governs and legislates for the good of humanity; and second, be willing to revise your views if someone presents a valid correction or argument, provided the change is grounded in justice or the common good, not merely in what seems pleasant or popular.

13. "Do you possess reason?" "I do." "Then why don't you use it? If reason fulfills its purpose, what more do you desire?"

14. You were born as part of the whole and will return to your Creator; or rather, you will be absorbed into His divine logic[1] through a transformative change.

15. Many grains of incense are offered on the same altar; one falls sooner, another later—it makes no difference.

16. Within ten days, those who now see you as a beast and an ape will regard you as a god—if you adhere to the principles and respect of Reason.

· · ·

17. Do not live as if you have ten thousand years ahead. Death is always near; while you live, as long as you can, be virtuous.

18. Great peace comes to the one who does not concern themselves with their neighbor's words, actions, or intentions—but focuses solely on their own deeds, ensuring they are just and virtuous. Do not be distracted, but proceed straight ahead, unwavering.

19. The person troubled by the thought of their legacy fails to realize that everyone who remembers them will soon pass away; and so it goes, until all memory fades, transferring from those who held it to those who let it go. Even if those who remember were immortal, and the memory itself everlasting—what does that matter to you? I'm not saying it's irrelevant to the deceased, but to the living, what is praise but perhaps a tool for good governance? For now, set aside that innate desire for recognition, which belongs to a different philosophy.

20. Anything truly beautiful is beautiful on its own and ends with itself, not relying on praise; it is neither diminished nor enhanced by it. This is true for things commonly deemed beautiful—like natural scenes and artworks. What does true beauty need? No more than law, truth, kindness, or respect. Which of these gains beauty from praise or loses value from criticism? Does an emerald become less if it is not praised? What about gold, ivory, purple fabrics, a lyre, a dagger, a flower, a young tree?

· · ·

21. If souls persist, how can the air accommodate them indefinitely? And how can the earth hold the bodies of those buried over millennia? Just as the decomposition and transformation of these bodies eventually make space for new ones, so too do souls that enter the air eventually change, disperse, and reignite into the universe's divine logic, making room for new souls. This is one way to address the question of eternal souls.

Yet, we must also think about the countless bodies buried and the multitude of creatures consumed daily by us and other animals. Despite the vast numbers consumed and in a sense buried within the predators, the earth absorbs them through the conversion to air or fire.

What, then, is the true belief on this matter? It involves understanding both the material and the efficient causes.

22. Do not let your mind wander. Instead, with every impulse, strive for justice, and with every thought, protect your ability to understand.

23. Everything is harmonious to me that aligns with you, O Universe. Nothing is too early or too late if it is timely for you. Everything is fruitful to me that your seasons yield, O Nature; from you all things emerge, in you all things exist, and to you all things return. Some may speak of "the beloved city of Cecrops"; wouldn't it be more apt to say, "The beloved city of Zeus"?

24. "Do only a few things if you wish for peace," so the saying goes. But isn't it better to do what is necessary, what the reasoning of a naturally social being dictates, and in the way it dictates? This not only brings the peace that comes from

virtuous actions but also the calm that comes from modest endeavors. Most of what we say and do is unnecessary. If we eliminate these, we make room for a life that is freer, less laborious, and untroubled. Therefore, we must constantly ask ourselves, "Is this unnecessary?" We should eliminate not just unnecessary actions but also idle thoughts; this way, no unnecessary actions will ensue.

25. Reflect on how the life of a virtuous person, who is content with what the universal laws provide, satisfied with their own moral actions, and possesses a kind disposition, would inspire you.

26. Having observed those things, now consider these. Do not let turmoil take hold of your soul; strive for tranquility. If someone commits a wrongdoing, the fault is theirs alone. If you encounter misfortune, it was destined from the start. Everything originates from the Source, connected to causes from eternity. In short, life is brief; we must cherish its present moments, guided by reason and justice. Remain composed and unshaken.

27. There exists either a well-ordered universe or a chaotic mix. Clearly, it is a universe; otherwise, how could there be order within you while chaos reigns outside? Especially when everything is so closely interconnected and in harmony?

28. Gloomy, effeminate, stubborn, animalistic, brutish, childish, lowly, deceitful, vulgar, enslaving, tyrannical.

· · ·

29. If someone is ignorant of what is foreign to the world, they are a stranger. Similarly, one who is unaware of the world's happenings is also a stranger. An exile is someone who rejects the law of reason; blind is the person who closes their mind's eye; impoverished is the one who depends on others without finding all that life requires within themselves; a sore on the world is someone who disconnects from our common nature's reason by resenting fate; for it brings forth what it has destined for you. A rebel against society is one who isolates their individual mind from the collective mind of all rational beings.

30. One philosopher goes without clothes, another without books. Here is one scantily clad: "I have no bread," he claims, "yet I adhere to reason." And I, lacking nourishment from learning, still cling to reason.

31. Cherish the art you have mastered, and find comfort in it. For the rest of your days, live as someone who has wholeheartedly entrusted their entire being to the gods; and regarding others, neither become a slave to anyone nor allow yourself to be enslaved.

32. Imagine the era of Vespasian. You'd observe the same human activities: marrying, raising families, falling ill, dying, engaging in wars, celebrating, trading, farming, flattering, displaying arrogance, harboring suspicions, scheming, wishing death upon others, complaining about their times, loving, accumulating wealth, and aspiring to high political positions. Yet, their era has vanished without a trace.

Shift your gaze to the times of Trajan. The story repeats

itself. That era, too, has faded away. Look through the annals of other periods and civilizations. Notice how many, after striving mightily, quickly faded away, dissolving back into the elements. Above all, consider those you have personally known. Those who, ignoring their true selves, clung stubbornly to something else, believing it sufficient. Remember, giving each action its due attention and weight is crucial. This way, you won't be disheartened by overemphasizing the trivial.

33. Words once common now sound archaic. Similarly, names of once-celebrated heroes like Camillus, Caeso, Volesus, Dentatus, and in time, Scipio and Cato, then Augustus, and eventually Hadrian and Antoninus, become relics of the past. All things swiftly transition into legend, then are engulfed by oblivion. This is true even for those who blazed brightly. For the rest, they are forgotten as soon as they pass away. What then is eternal memory? Merely an illusion. What should we then focus on? Only this: a mind aligned with justice, deeds beneficial to all, truthful speech, and an acceptance of everything that occurs as necessary, familiar, and originating from the same universal source.

34. Embrace your fate with willingness, letting Clotho[2] spin your destiny as she sees fit.

35. Both the rememberer and the remembered are fleeting.

36. Recognize that all things emerge through transformation. Train yourself to see that Nature delights in changing existing

forms and creating new ones in their likeness. Everything in existence can be seen as a seed for what will come next. Yet, if you think seeds are only those things planted in soil or born from a womb, you're viewing it too narrowly.

37. Your time is short, and yet you haven't achieved simplicity, tranquility, immunity to the perceived harm of external things, kindness towards everyone, nor have you understood that true wisdom lies in just action.

38. Understand the nature of those whose approval you seek and the objectives they chase or avoid.

39. Your troubles don't stem from someone else's influence or any change in your physical condition. So where do they lie? In the part of you that judges what is good or bad. Stop making such judgments, and you'll be fine. Even if your body suffers - cut, burned, festering, or decaying - let the part of you that judges remain calm, recognizing that nothing that affects both the virtuous and the wicked equally can be deemed good or bad. What happens to both the just and the unjust alike is neither natural nor unnatural.

40. Reflect on the universe as a living entity, composed of a single substance and soul. Think about how everything merges into this collective consciousness, how it's guided by a unified force, and how every event is intricately linked, forming a complex, interwoven tapestry.

. . .

41. As Epictetus would say, you are but a tiny soul carrying around a corpse.

42. Change is neither bad nor good; it's simply a part of existence.

43. Time is a relentless river, swiftly carrying away everything in its path. No sooner does something appear than it is gone, replaced by the next thing in the ceaseless flow.

44. Every occurrence is as common and predictable as roses blooming in spring or fruit ripening in summer. This includes disease, death, defamation, intrigue, and all that delights or distresses the uninformed.

45. What happens next is always logically linked to what happened before. It's not just a random series of events, but a logical progression. Just as things in existence are perfectly synchronized, so are the events that unfold, exhibiting not just continuity but a remarkable interconnection.

46. Remember Heraclitus' insight that earth transforms into water, water into air, air into fire, and then reverses. Recall his metaphor of the man who forgets his destination; how people conflict with the very logic they live by daily, finding it foreign; that we shouldn't live as if we're dreaming (even though we often do); and that we must not mimic children who parrot their parents, but think and speak for ourselves.

. . .

47. Imagine a deity informs you that you'll die tomorrow or the day after. You wouldn't fret much over the exact day unless you valued life too lightly. What does it matter if you die tomorrow or in many years?

48. Constantly remind yourself of how many doctors, astrologers, philosophers, warriors, and tyrants have passed away, despite their professions or power. Remember cities like Helice, Pompeii, Herculaneum, and others that have vanished. Reflect on everyone you've known who has died.

This teaches us to view life as fleeting and insignificant. We go from being unborn to dust or ashes in a moment.

Live harmoniously with nature during this brief existence, leaving it willingly, like a ripe olive falling to the ground, thanking the earth that nurtured it and the tree that allowed it to flourish.

49. Be like the headland against which the waves continually crash, yet it stands firm and tames the fury of the water around it.

"Woe is me, that this has befallen me." Not so, but rather, "Fortunate am I, that though this has happened to me, I continue untroubled, neither crushed by the present nor fearing the future." For such an event could have happened to anyone, but not everyone could have remained untroubled in such circumstances. Why then is the one considered a misfortune rather than the other counted a blessing? Can you truly call something a human misfortune which does not deviate from human nature? And does it seem to you a deviation from human nature, when it is not contrary to the will of that nature? Well then, you have learned that will. Does this event prevent you from being just, magnanimous, temperate, prudent, secure against rash opinions and falsehood, modest, free, and all else which enables human nature to maintain its proper character? Remember henceforth in every situation that causes you vexation to apply this principle: that this is not misfortune, but to bear it nobly is good fortune.

50. A common but effective aid to dismissing the fear of death is to consider those who have desperately clung to life. What more have they achieved than those who died early? Eventually, they all lie the same—Caedicianus, Fabius, Julianus, Lepidus, or any other such, who led many to their graves and then were themselves carried to their own. The interval between birth and death is brief, filled with troubles, spent in the company of certain people, and in a fragile body! Therefore, do not regard life as something of great value. For consider the vast expanse of time behind you, and the time which lies ahead, another boundless space. In this infinity, what difference does it make whether one lives for three days or three generations?

51. Always take the short path; and the short path is the natural one: thus, say and do everything in accordance with the soundest reason. For this approach frees a person from trouble, strife, all pretense, and ostentatious display.

BOOK 5

1. AT DAWN, WHEN YOU STRUGGLE TO GET OUT OF BED, TELL yourself: "I am rising to do the work of a human being. Why am I complaining if I am going to do what I was born for—the things I was brought into the world to do? Or was I created just to lie in bed and keep myself warm?" "But this is more pleasant." So, were you born for mere pleasure: in general, were you born for sensation or for action? Don't you see the plants, the sparrows, the ants, the spiders, the bees working together to organize their separate parts of the universe? And yet you don't want to do the work of a human being, and you don't rush to do what is according to your nature? "But rest is necessary too." It is necessary. However, nature has set limits to this as well, just as it has to eating and drinking, and yet you exceed these limits, beyond what is sufficient. But with your duties, you fall short of what you are capable of. So you do not love yourself, or else you would love your nature and her will.

But those who love their crafts toil at them unwashed and without food. But you honor your own nature less than the engraver values the art of engraving, or the dancer the art of dancing, or the lover of money values his wealth, or the vainglorious man his fleeting glory. And such individuals, when they have a deep passion for something, choose neither to eat nor to sleep rather than to perfect the things they care for. But are the acts that concern society less noble in your eyes and less worthy of your effort?

2. It is easy to dismiss every troubling or unfit thought and find oneself in complete calm.

3. Consider yourself deserving of every word and action that aligns with nature. Let not the disapproval or criticism of others deter you. If it's right to speak or act, don't deem yourself unworthy. Others have their guiding principles and follow their impulses, which shouldn't concern you. Instead, proceed directly, guided by your own and the universal nature, for both paths are one.

4. I follow nature's path until I lay down to rest, breathing my last into the source of my daily breath, returning to the earth from which my father drew the seed, my mother the blood, and my nurse the milk; the earth that has nourished and hydrated me for years, borne my footsteps, and served countless purposes for me.

5. They may not admire your sharp wit—so be it. Yet, you possess many other qualities that cannot be dismissed as natural shortcomings. Exhibit those fully within your control: honesty, dignity, perseverance, simplicity, satisfaction with your fate, frugality, kindness, independence, straightforwardness, gravity,

and generosity. Can you not see the multitude of virtues you can show without blaming a lack of talent? And still, you choose to live below your potential? Does a supposed lack of talent justify your complaints, stinginess, flattery, self-deprecation, obsequiousness, boastfulness, and inner turmoil? Certainly not! You could have overcome these long ago. If you are indeed slow to understand, work on it without indulging in or enjoying your sluggishness.

6. Some people, after doing a good deed, quickly consider it a favor owed to them. Others may not think of it so immediately but still see the recipient as indebted, aware of their generosity. A third kind scarcely acknowledges their good actions, resembling a vine that produces grapes and seeks nothing more once it yields its fruit.

Like a horse that has raced, a dog that has hunted, or a bee that has made honey, a person who has performed a good deed does not boast but moves on to the next task, as a vine produces grapes again when the season returns. Aim to be someone who does good almost without noticing.

—Indeed, but one must recognize this very fact, for it's inherent in a social creature to understand when he is acting for the common good and, indeed, to desire acknowledgment from his peers.

—Your point is valid, but you misunderstand the essence of this teaching. By doing so, you risk being like those previously mentioned, even though they are deceived by seemingly sound logic. However, if you strive to grasp the meaning of these words, fear not that you will neglect any social duty.

· · ·

7. REFLECT ON THE ATHENIANS' Prayer: "Rain, rain, O dear Zeus, on the fields and plains of Athens." One should either refrain from praying or pray in this simple and noble way.

8. When it is said, "Asclepius prescribed horseback riding, cold baths, or walking barefoot for this man," it's akin to saying, "Universal Nature prescribed illness, mutilation, loss, or something similar for this man." In the former, "prescribed" means he ordered it for health; in the latter, what happens to each person is deemed suitable for his fate.

We say such events "befall" us, just as stonemasons say squared blocks "come together" in walls or pyramids, fitting in a specific arrangement. There's a harmony overall, and just as the cosmos is composed of all bodies to form such a body, so is destiny composed of all causes to form such a cause.

Even those with minimal education grasp this, saying, "This was his fate." Thus, it was brought to him and ordained for him. Let's accept these things as we accept what Asclepius prescribes —for many of his prescriptions are harsh, yet we welcome them hoping for health.

Similarly, regard the fulfillment of what seems best to Universal Nature as akin to your health, and thus welcome all that happens, even if stern, because it leads you to that goal—the health of the cosmos, the prosperity and well-being of Zeus. He wouldn't bring this upon anyone if it weren't for the good of the whole. Nor does any nature produce what isn't in harmony with its governance.

Therefore, there are two reasons to be content with your fate: first, because it happened to you, was prescribed for you, and woven into your destiny from eternity; and second, because what happens to each is a cause of the prosperity, perfection, and coherence of the whole. The integrity of the whole is compromised if any connection, no matter how small, is severed. And you do sever this connection, as far as you can, whenever you're discontent, thereby damaging it.

9. Do not feel disgust, discouragement, or displeasure if you don't always act from right principles; but when thwarted, return to them, and rejoice if overall your conduct is worthy of a human being, and love that to which you return. Don't approach philosophy as if it were a strict teacher, but as the bleary-eyed come to a sponge and an egg, as another comes to a poultice, or to a fomentation.

In this way, you won't be "obeying reason" as an imposition, but will find rest in it. Remember, too, that philosophy desires only what your nature wants; whereas you desired something against nature. Which is more appealing? Pleasure deceives us for this very reason. But consider whether magnanimity, freedom, simplicity, equanimity, and piety are not more appealing. And what is more appealing than wisdom itself, when you consider its unhampered fluency of intelligence and knowledge in all things?

10. The essence of the universe is so deeply veiled in mystery that numerous philosophers—renowned ones at that—have deemed it utterly beyond understanding. Even the Stoics, with their profound insights, struggle to grasp it fully. Our judgments are always prone to change, for who among us has never altered their perspective? Hence, focus on the nature of things themselves: how fleeting, insignificant, and vulnerable they are, easily falling under the control of the corrupt and the wicked. Then, reflect on the nature of those we share our lives with—enduring

even the most pleasant company can be a challenge, let alone coping with one's own flaws.

Amidst such obscurity and degradation, in a world constantly in flux—where time, movement, and change are omnipresent—what truly deserves to be valued or taken seriously? I find nothing. Instead, we should find solace in awaiting our natural end, not resenting the wait but taking comfort in these thoughts alone: first, that nothing will occur to me that doesn't align with the universal nature; and second, that it's within my power to act in harmony with my conscience and inner guide, for no one can force me to act against it.

11. How am I employing my soul at this moment? This is the question I must ponder continuously, asking: What is the current state of that part of me known as the ruling principle? Is my soul now that of a child, a young person, a weak individual, a tyrant, a tame creature, or a wild animal?

12. You can gauge what the masses consider valuable by this observation. Suppose someone regards qualities like wisdom, temperance, justice, and bravery as truly valuable. Having embraced these virtues, that person would find the poet's phrase "by his goods" irrelevant. However, if one first values what the masses deem important and then hears the poet's phrase, it would seem fitting. Thus, even the masses distinguish between genuine and superficial values. Otherwise, the verse wouldn't be offensive or dismissed when we find it apt and cleverly used in the context of wealth, luxury, or fame. Therefore, continue to question whether we should esteem things that, when first considered, would make the crude remark about being so well-off that one "has no place to defecate" seem appropriate[1].

. . .

13. I consist of a causal and a material component. Neither will cease to exist, just as neither emerged from nothing. Thus, every part of me will, through transformation, contribute to some aspect of the universe, and that part will, in turn, transform into another aspect ad infinitum. It is through such transformations that I came into being, as did my ancestors, stretching back endlessly. This process continues unimpeded, even if the universe operates in finite cycles.

14. Reason and the art of reasoning are self-sufficient, content solely with their own operations. They start from their own premises and move towards their intended outcomes; such actions are termed "right conduct" because they indicate the correctness of the path chosen.

15. None of these attributes should be considered inherent to being human, as they do not naturally occur to someone simply because they are human. They are not essential to human nature, nor does human nature guarantee them, nor do they enhance human nature. Hence, the ultimate goal of being human isn't found in these attributes, nor in what completes this goal, the good. For if any of these attributes were inherent to humans, despising them and striving to be above them wouldn't be appropriate, nor would someone who seeks independence from them be commendable. Similarly, someone who devalues themselves in relation to these attributes wouldn't be considered good if these attributes were indeed good. In reality, the more a person renounces these or similar things, or even tolerates their absence, the better they become.

. . .

16. Your mind will take on the form of what you consistently visualize. For the soul is colored by its impressions. Therefore, paint it with continuous thoughts like these: wherever life is possible, a good life is possible too. Since one can live in a palace, it follows that one can also live well in a palace. Moreover, everything is created with a purpose and moves towards fulfilling that purpose; its end is in that direction, and there lies each thing's benefit and goodness. Thus, the good of a rational being lies in community. It has long been established that we are meant for communal life. Isn't it evident that lesser entities serve the greater, and the greater serve each other? Beings with souls are superior to those without, and those with reason surpass those with souls alone.

17. Chasing the impossible is folly; it is impossible for wicked people not to act reprehensibly.

18. Nothing happens to anyone that they are not naturally equipped to handle. Others face the same challenges and, either out of ignorance or a desire to demonstrate their resilience, remain steadfast and unscathed. Therefore, it is disgraceful for ignorance and vanity to triumph over wisdom.

19. External factors cannot touch the soul, gain access to it, alter it, or move it. The soul alone changes and moves itself, and it forms judgments it deems suitable under the circumstances.

. . .

20. In one respect, humans are our closest relatives, as we are obligated to assist and bear with them. However, when some impede our rightful deeds, they become as indifferent to us as the sun, wind, or a wild animal. These may obstruct certain activities, but they cannot impede our will or disposition, thanks to our ability to make reservations and adapt. The mind transforms every obstacle into an opportunity, turning a roadblock into assistance and an impediment into progress.

21. Honor the mightiest force in the cosmos—that which wields power over all and governs everything. Similarly, honor the mightiest force within you—that which resonates with the cosmic power. For it is this force within you that controls everything else and guides your life.

22. If something does not harm the community, it does not harm the individual. When you feel wronged, consider this: if the community is not harmed, then neither am I. If the community is harmed, anger is not the answer; instead, gently correct the wrongdoer, pointing out their disregard for the community's well-being.

23. Often reflect on how quickly everything in existence is swept away. Substance is like a river in constant flow, its actions ever changing, its causes infinitely varied, and almost nothing remains static—even things close at hand. Consider also the vast expanse of time past and future, into which all things disappear. How foolish, then, to be arrogant, troubled, or to make a spectacle, as if these things could affect one for long.

·　·　·

24. Remember the entirety of matter, of which you are but a tiny fragment; the entirety of time, of which you experience only a brief moment; and destiny, of which you play such a small part.

25. If someone wrongs me, that is their issue; they have their own character and actions. What nature intends for me now, I possess; what nature intends for me to do now, I do.

26. Let the dominant and sovereign part of your soul remain unaffected by bodily sensations, whether pleasant or unpleasant. It should not mix with them, but instead set boundaries and confine these sensations to their respective body parts. However, when these sensations reach the mind due to the body's interconnectedness, it's natural to feel them, but the dominant part of the mind must not judge them as either good or bad.

27. "TO LIVE WITH THE GODS." One lives with the gods by showing them a soul satisfied with its fate and executing the will of the guardian spirit—a piece of Zeus given to each person as a guide and overseer, which is nothing other than one's intelligence and reason.

28. Are you upset with someone because of their bad breath or body odor? What can they do about it? Their mouth and armpits are the sources—it's natural for these odors to emanate from there. "But they have the faculty of reason," you might say, "and upon reflection, can see where they go wrong." Excellent point! You too possess reason. Use your rationality to awaken

theirs; enlighten and remind them. If they heed your advice, you'll have helped them, and there will be no need for anger.

Do not be a tragic actor[2] nor a prostitute[3].

29. Live as you intend to when you leave this world, and if that's not allowed, then leave life as though you're suffering no harm. "There's smoke, and I'm leaving. Why make a big deal out of it?" But until something forces me out, I remain free. No one can stop me from doing as I please—that is, to live as a rational and social being.

30. The universe's mind is inherently social. It created lesser things for the sake of the greater and made the greater things complement each other. Observe how it has organized, coordinated, and assigned everything its rightful place, achieving harmony among the best of things.

31. Reflect on how you've treated the gods, your parents, siblings, spouse, children, teachers, mentors, friends, relatives, and servants. Ask yourself if you've lived so that it can be said of you:

"He never wronged anyone in action or speech."

Remember all you've experienced, what you've endured, and that your life's story is now complete, your service concluded. Think of the beautiful sights you've seen, the pleasures and pains you've overlooked, the honors you've refused, and the kindness you've shown to those with ill intentions.

· · ·

32. Why do those who lack skill and knowledge confuse those who are skilled and wise? Which soul then possesses skill and knowledge? The one that understands the beginning and the end, the logic that permeates all matter, and governs the universe through fixed periods.

33. Soon you will be ashes or bones, a name or perhaps not even that; but a name is just sound and echo. The things highly prized in life are insubstantial, decaying, and petty, like little dogs snapping at each other, and children fighting, laughing, then immediately crying. Yet, integrity, humility, justice, and truth have ascended

"To Olympus from the widespread earth."

What keeps you here, if sensory objects are fleeting and unstable, sensory organs are unreliable, and the soul itself is but a vapor from blood? To seek fame in such a world is vain. Why not wait peacefully for your end, whether it be dissolution or transformation? Until then, what is enough? Nothing but to respect and thank the gods, to be kind to humans, to practice patience and self-control; and regarding all beyond the reach of our frail body and breath, to remember it is neither ours nor under our control.

34. You can live in continuous happiness if you find and follow the right path in thought and action. These qualities are shared by the divine soul, the human soul, and every rational being: not to be impeded by others; and to find fulfillment in a commitment to justice and its practice.

.   .   .

35. If this situation isn't due to my own fault or a consequence of my wrongdoing, and the common good isn't harmed, why should I be troubled? And how is the common good harmed?

36. Don't let your imagination carry you away, but offer help where you can and when it's appropriate. Even if others are at a disadvantage in trivial matters, don't see it as harmful; that's a negative mindset. Just as an old man, upon departing, asked for his foster child's spinning top, remembering it was just a toy—so should you remember. Since you excel in public speaking, have you forgotten the significance of these trivial matters? To them, these issues matter deeply. Will you then act foolishly on account of this?

I once found myself fortunate wherever fate took me. And being fortunate means creating your own good fortune. Good fortunes are positive states of mind, constructive impulses, and noble deeds.

BOOK 6

1. THE ESSENCE OF THE UNIVERSE IS MALLEABLE AND COMPLIANT, and the logic that guides it harbors no intention to harm. It lacks malice, never acts with ill intent, and causes no harm. Everything unfolds and concludes according to its purpose.

2. It matters not whether you act rightly while cold or warm, sleepy or alert, criticized or praised, dying or engaged in any other activity. For death, too, is a part of life, and even in death, it is enough to live the present moment well.

3. Look within. Do not overlook the unique nature or value of anything.

4. All things will soon transform, either vanishing as vapor if all is one substance, or scattering.

. . .

5. The guiding intelligence is aware of its own nature, its actions, and the material it shapes.

6. The best revenge is not to become like the one who wronged you.

7. Find joy and peace in one thing alone: transitioning from one act of community to another, with the divine in mind.

8. The mind is what awakens and transforms itself, shaping its perceptions and making everything that occurs seem as it wishes.

9. Everything unfolds according to the universe's nature, for nothing happens according to any external imposition, containment, or detachment.

10. It is either chaos, a tangle, and disintegration—or unity, order, and design. If the former, why desire to remain in such confusion? Why care about anything other than my eventual return to the earth? Why be troubled? Disintegration will claim me regardless. But if the latter is true, I respect it, stand by it, and place my trust in the governing force.

11. When circumstances force you into disturbance, quickly realign with your inner self and deviate from your rhythm no

more than necessary. You'll better maintain harmony by consistently returning to it.

12. If you had both a stepmother and a mother, you would honor the former, but you would always return to your mother. The court and philosophy are like this for you now. Frequently return and find solace in philosophy, through which your experiences in the court also become tolerable, and you remain composed under those conditions.

13. Think of food and delicacies this way: envision the fish as a dead body, the bird or pig as a carcass. Falernian wine is just fermented grape juice, and that luxurious purple-edged robe is merely sheep's wool dyed with the blood of shellfish. Sexual intercourse? It's nothing more than the rubbing together of organs and the release of some fluid. These perspectives cut through to the essence of things, revealing their true nature. This is how you should approach life: stripping away the veneer from things that seem significant, exposing their insignificance, and peeling back the myths that inflate their value. Conceit is a master of illusion, especially when you believe you're focused on what's important. That's when you're most susceptible. Reflect on what Crates said about Xenocrates[1].

14. The things that most people admire fall into basic categories —objects bound by natural forces like stones, wood, fig trees, vines, and olives. Those with slightly more discernment value things animated by life, such as livestock. Those with even finer tastes appreciate manifestations of the rational soul, not in its universal aspect, but for its skill, artistry, or talent, such as

owning numerous slaves. However, someone who truly values the rational soul—in its universal and civic-minded form—dismisses these lesser concerns. Their primary aim is to maintain their own soul in a state of rationality, sociability, and alignment with the divine.

15. Some things rush into existence, others rush to depart. Even as something comes into being, part of it is already fading away. Continuous change and movement rejuvenate the world, just as the unending passage of time keeps eternity eternally youthful. In the swiftly flowing river of existence, what is there to hold dear? It's akin to becoming attached to a sparrow darting by, only for it to disappear from view. Such is the life of every person—like the drawing of a breath and its release. The act of breathing, in and out, mirrors the cycle of life itself: drawing in life's breath as a newborn only to return it at death.

16. Humans are distinguished from plants by not merely growing, from animals by not just breathing, from inanimate objects by not being moved solely by external forces, from puppets by not being jerked around by impulses, from herds by not gathering solely for sustenance. Even the act of eating, which mirrors excretion, is not what should be honored. Is it applause we seek? No, not even the applause of many, for that is just noise. Having abandoned the pursuit of fame, what then is worthy? It is to act and to be restrained in a manner true to our own nature, a goal to which the practice of any art also aspires.

Every art strives for its creation to be fit for its purpose. Whether it's the vine-dresser tending the vines, the horse-breaker, or the dog-trainer, all aim for this outcome. Education and teaching aim for the same. This is where true value lies, and if this is achieved, nothing else will be sought after. Will you not then disregard many other things? If not, you will not be free, self-sufficient, or free from passion. You will inevitably feel envy, jealousy, and suspicion towards those who can deprive you of these things, and harbor resentment towards those who possess what you desire. In essence, anyone who needs these things will be in constant turmoil, always blaming the gods.

But by valuing and respecting your own mind, you will find contentment within yourself, live in harmony with others, and be in accord with the gods—celebrating all they provide and decree.

17. The elements move up, down, and in circles, but the motion of virtue is in none of these—it is something more divine, following a path that's hard to see, yet it ultimately thrives.

18. It's odd what people do. They withhold praise from those around them, yet they value being praised by future generations they'll never meet. This is almost as ridiculous as being upset that past generations didn't praise you.

19. Don't assume that if something is difficult for you to master, it's impossible for anyone. Instead, if something is possible and appropriate for a person, believe it's achievable for you too.

20. In the gym, someone might accidentally scratch us or bump into us, but we don't get upset, take offense, or suspect them of malice. We maintain our distance, yes, but without bitterness or distrust, simply steering clear with goodwill. Apply this

approach to other aspects of life: forgive many things in those who are, in a way, your training partners. It's possible to avoid them without suspicion or animosity.

21. If anyone can prove me wrong and point out my mistake in any thought or action, I will happily change. I seek the truth, which never harmed anyone: the real harm lies in persisting in one's own delusion and ignorance.

22. I focus on my duties. Other things don't distract me because they are either inanimate, irrational, or have lost their way and are unaware of the right path.

23. Treat irrational animals, and generally things and objects, with generosity and liberty, as a rational being ought to treat things lacking reason. Treat humans, as rational beings, with friendliness. In all situations, call upon the gods. And don't worry about how long you will do this. Even three hours spent this way is enough.

24. Alexander the Great and his mule driver both died and ended up in the same condition, for either they were absorbed back into the universal source of life, or they were both scattered into atoms.

25. Think about how many activities happen within each of us at the same moment—things both physical and mental. Then you won't be surprised if many more things, indeed all things that

exist in the unity and vastness we call the universe, occur simultaneously.

26. If someone asks you how to spell 'Antoninus', would you shout each letter? What if they became angry? Would you respond with anger? Wouldn't you rather spell out each letter calmly? Similarly, remember that every duty consists of specific steps. Pay attention to these and, without getting upset or angry at those who are angry with you, methodically complete the task at hand.

27. It's cruel to prevent people from pursuing what they believe is right and beneficial for them. Yet, in a way, you do just that when you resent their misdeeds. They are undoubtedly acting on what they think is right and beneficial.—"But it's not."—Then teach and show them the right way without resentment.

28. Death offers relief from the relentless onslaught of senses, the involuntary twitching of impulses, the wandering mind, and the demands of the body.

29. It is disgraceful for the soul to give up while the body still endures.

30. Guard against becoming imperial, adopting that tint—for it is a real possibility. Stay simple, virtuous, pure, earnest, unpretentious, a champion of justice, devout, compassionate, affectionate, and robust in your designated work. Aim to

remain as philosophy intended you to be. Honor the gods, care for humanity. Life is fleeting; the true reward of our earthly journey is a virtuous character and deeds that benefit society.

Follow the example of Antoninus in all things. Emulate his unwavering commitment to rational action, his steady composure, his devoutness, his calm demeanor, his kindness, his indifference to vanity, and his dedication to understanding matters fully.

Recall how he never dismissed anything without thorough examination and clear comprehension; how he endured unjust criticism without retaliating; how he never acted impulsively; how he ignored slander; how meticulously he assessed people and their deeds; he was not a critic, coward, skeptic, or sophist. Remember how little he needed—in terms of housing, bedding, attire, food, servants.

Consider his diligence and patience; how his modest diet allowed him to wait until evening to relieve himself, without needing to at unusual times. Reflect on his consistency and fairness in friendships; how he welcomed honest dissent and appreciated being corrected; how devout he was without being superstitious. Ponder all these things so that when your time comes, you may face it with a conscience as clear as his.

31. Clear your head and reclaim your senses. Once awake, recognize that what troubled you were merely dreams, and now that you are alert, regard these realities as you did those dreams.

32. I am but a simple body and soul. To the body, all things are neutral, for it cannot engage with them. To the soul, only its own actions matter; and of these, it has control. Furthermore, it is

only concerned with the present moment; what is past or yet to come is irrelevant now.

33. Work is not a burden for the hand or foot when each performs its designated task and no more; likewise, it is not a burden for a person. If it is natural for a person, it is not harmful.

34. Consider the pleasures enjoyed by bandits, deviants, murderers, and tyrants!

35. Do you not see how craftsmen, while somewhat accommodating the layperson, still adhere strictly to the tenets of their trade and cannot bear to deviate from them? Isn't it odd that architects and doctors respect the principles of their professions more than a human being respects his own principles, which he shares with the gods?

36. Asia and Europe are but corners of the universe; every ocean a mere droplet within it; Mount Athos, just a speck of dirt; the present moment, a fleeting instant in eternity. Everything is minute, transient, and easily altered.

All things originate from the same universal mind—either as a result or by direct intention. Thus, the lion's gaping jaws, poison, and all that harms—like thorns or mud—are offshoots of the grand and the beautiful. Do not view these elements as foreign to what you hold dear, but reflect on their origins.

· · ·

37. One who sees the present has seen everything—everything that has ever happened since the dawn of time and everything that will happen forevermore. For all things share the same essence and form.

38. Regularly reflect on the interconnectedness of all things in the universe and their relationship to one another. For in a sense, everything is intertwined, making all things fond of each other. This is due to the tensional forces, the shared breath of life, and the unity of all matter.

39. Embrace the life that fate has given you, and genuinely cherish the people with whom fate has decided you should live.

40. A tool or utensil, if it fulfills the purpose for which it was made, is considered effective, even if its maker is no longer around. However, for things created by nature, the force that formed them remains and persists within. Therefore, you should hold it in even higher regard, believing that living in harmony with its purpose will ensure that everything in your life will unfold as it should. This applies to the universe as well, which operates perfectly according to its own nature.

41. When you regard things beyond your control as either good or bad, you inevitably find yourself blaming the gods and resenting those believed to be responsible for any misfortune or loss. This often leads to unjust actions. However, if we consider only what is within our control as good or evil, there is no basis for grievances against the divine or hostility towards others.

. . .

42. We are all contributors to a common goal, some of us knowingly and intentionally, others without awareness. As Heraclitus suggests, even those who are asleep participate in the workings of the universe. Each contributes in their own unique way; even those who complain or seek to oppose the natural order play a significant role. The universe needs such individuals too. It's up to you to decide which type of contributor you wish to be. The governing force of the universe will surely find a use for you and welcome you among its collaborators. Just ensure you're not what Chrysippus referred to as a useless and absurd character in the play.

43. Does the sun attempt to perform the role of the rain? Or Asclepius that of Demeter? And what about the stars? While they vary in brilliance, do they not all work together towards a common purpose?

44. Now, if the gods have made plans regarding my fate, they have surely made them wisely, for it is hard to envision a god lacking in wisdom. But why would they wish me harm? What benefit would that bring to them or to the universe, which is their primary concern? If they haven't considered my case specifically, they have definitely thought about the general good, and I should gladly accept whatever results from that.

If, by some chance, they don't concern themselves with anything at all (a blasphemous thought, which would render our sacrifices, prayers, oaths, and all acts of worship meaningless), then the responsibility falls to me to consider my own welfare. The well-being of any entity is in aligning with its nature and essence. My essence is rational and social.

As Antoninus, my city and fatherland is Rome; as a human, it is the universe. Only what benefits these communities is truly good for me.

45. Whatever happens to an individual contributes to the welfare of the whole. This principle should be enough, yet upon closer examination, you'll find that what benefits one often benefits others as well. However, let's apply the term "good" in a broader sense, encompassing things of a neutral nature.

46. Just as the repeated performances in the amphitheater become dull from their sameness, so does life when viewed as a whole; everything, both grand and trivial, originates from the same source and follows the same patterns. How long, then, can this go on?

47. Often think of the multitude of people from different walks of life and from various nations who have died, extending your thoughts to include Philistion, Phoebus, and Origanion. Then consider other groups of humanity. We must remember those who have gone before us, including the great orators, the revered philosophers like Heraclitus, Pythagoras, Socrates, the ancient heroes, the generals and rulers of later eras. Also, remember figures like Eudoxus, Hipparchus, Archimedes, and other brilliant, ambitious, ingenious, and proud individuals, as well as those who ridiculed the fleeting nature of human life, like Menippus and his ilk. Understand that all these individuals have long since

passed away. What harm has it brought them? And what of it for those whose names are even forgotten? Here, one thing holds immense value: to live your life with truth and fairness, showing kindness even to those who are deceitful and unjust.

48. When in need of uplift, think of the virtues of your companions—the vigor of one, the modesty of another, the generosity of a third, and so on. Nothing is as heartening as the collective display of virtues in the people around you. Thus, keep these reflections readily accessible.

49. Are you upset because you only weigh so much and not three hundred pounds? Then why not also be upset that you're only given so many years to live and not more? Just as you accept the amount of matter assigned to you, you should also accept the time you've been given.

50. Try to persuade others, but if justice demands, act against their will. If someone forcefully opposes you, find another way, remain calm, and turn the obstacle into a chance to practice a different virtue. Remember, you started this journey with certain conditions, not aiming for the impossible. What then? A noble effort. And this you achieve, even when faced with obstacles.

51. The ambitious see another's success as their fortune; the pleasure-seeker, his sensations; but the wise, his actions.

· · ·

52. You can choose not to form opinions on this matter and thus maintain your peace of mind, for things themselves don't have the power to dictate our judgments.

53. Make it a habit to listen attentively to others, trying as much as possible to understand the speaker's perspective.

54. What harms the hive harms the bee.

55. If sailors insulted the helmsman or patients berated their doctor, would they heed anyone else? How then could the helmsman ensure the passengers' safety or the doctor the health of his patients?

56. How many who were born into this world with me have already left it!

57. To someone with jaundice, honey tastes bitter; to someone with rabies, water is terrifying; to children, a ball is a marvel. So why am I upset? Do you think the mind's false impressions have less impact than jaundice or rabies?

58. No one can prevent you from living according to your own rational nature; nothing will happen to you that goes against the rational nature of the universe.

· · ·

59. Reflect on what people are like when they eat, sleep, mate, defecate, and so forth. Then consider what they become when they're commanding or arrogant, or when they're angry and shouting from their high horses. Not long ago, how many were they subservient to, and for what? And soon, what will become of them?

BOOK 7

1. What is evil? It's what you've seen time and again. Whenever something happens, remember that it's nothing new. You'll find the same things everywhere, in ancient stories, in recent times, and today; in cities and homes. There's nothing new under the sun: all things are familiar and fleeting.

2. How can our principles die if the thoughts that correspond to them are alive? It's within your power to keep these thoughts ablaze. I can hold any opinion by choice. If so, why am I upset? External things have no bearing on my mind. Maintain this attitude, and you will stand tall.

Reclaiming your life is within your power. Look at things as you once did; this is how you recover your life.

3. The allure of grandeur, theatrical performances, herds of animals, tournaments, a bone thrown to small dogs, a piece of food tossed into fishponds, the laborious efforts of ants, the

frantic scampering of frightened mice, and puppets pulled by strings—all amidst this, one must remain kind-hearted and humble, recognizing that a person's value is equivalent to what they dedicate themselves to.

4. Listen intently to what is said and observe closely what happens at every moment. In the case of actions, quickly identify the intention behind them. In the case of words, thoughtfully interpret their meaning.

5. Is my intellect up to this task? If so, I use it as a tool provided by the universe to complete the work. If not, I either hand over the task to someone more capable—if that is the appropriate action—or I do what I can, seeking assistance from someone who, under my guidance, can achieve what is currently necessary and beneficial for the community. Whatever I do, whether on my own or with help, I aim solely at what is useful and appropriate for the collective.

6. Reflect on how many once celebrated individuals are now forgotten, and how many who sang their praises have long since vanished.

7. Do not feel embarrassed to be assisted, for your duty is to fulfill your role, like a soldier storming a fortress. What if you, hindered by a disability, cannot climb the walls alone, but could with someone else's help?

· · ·

8. Do not let the future unsettle you, for you will face it, if need be, with the same reasoning you apply to current matters.

9. All things are interconnected, and this bond is sacred; hardly anything is completely unrelated to another. Everything has been organized into its rightful place and together beautifies the universe. For there is one universe composed of all things, one God throughout all, one substance, one law, one rationality shared by all thinking beings, and one truth—if indeed there is also one ideal for all entities of the same nature, sharing the same logic.

10. Everything physical quickly dissolves into the cosmic whole, and every cause is rapidly absorbed back into the universal logic; the memory of everything is swiftly entombed in eternity.

11. For a rational being, acting according to nature and logic is the same.

12. Upright on one's own, not propped up.

13. Just as the limbs of a body are united in one system, so are rational beings, though distinct, designed to work together. This realization becomes more profound if you frequently remind yourself, "I am a limb of the collective of rational beings." However, if you consider yourself merely a "part," you have not yet learned to love humanity deeply. Doing good has not yet

become a joy in itself for you; you still view it as an obligation, not yet as a kindness to yourself.

14. Let external events impact those who are susceptible to them. If they choose, they might complain about their fate, but as for me, if I don't label what has occurred as evil, I remain unharmed. It's within my control not to make such an assumption.

15. No matter what anyone does or says, I must remain virtuous, just like gold, emerald, or purple consistently reminds itself: "No matter what anyone does or says, I must remain emerald and keep my color."

16. The mind does not disturb itself; it doesn't frighten or desire on its own accord. If others can provoke fear or pain, let them; the mind, based on its own judgments, will not engage in such emotions. Let the body fend for itself and speak if it suffers; but the soul—the part that feels fear, grief, and makes judgments— will remain unaffected, as long as you don't force it to judge otherwise. The mind, in its essence, is self-sufficient and calm, unless it disrupts itself.

17. True happiness lies in a benevolent spirit or a well-guided mind. So why are you here, imagination? Leave, by the gods, as you arrived; I have no need for you. You've returned out of habit. I'm not upset with you; just leave.

· · ·

18. Is the idea of change frightening? But how can anything come into existence without change? What's more natural or essential to the universe than change? Can you enjoy a hot bath without wood transforming by fire? Can you be nourished without your food changing? Can anything useful be achieved without change? See, then, that your own change is just as necessary for the universe.

19. Like a rushing torrent, the universal substance carries all bodies, naturally connected and cooperating with the whole, just as our limbs work together. Time has already claimed many a Chrysippus, Socrates, and Epictetus. Apply this thought to every person and thing.

20. Only one thing troubles me: that I may act against what humanity requires, in a manner it doesn't desire, or at a time it doesn't need.

21. Soon, you will forget all things; and soon, all will forget you.

22. It is uniquely human to love even those who err. This becomes apparent when you realize they are kin, erring out of ignorance and without intent, and that soon both of you will pass away; and most importantly, that the one who wronged you hasn't damaged your ability to think and judge correctly.

23. The universe molds existence much like wax, creating a small horse one moment, melting it down, and from that same

substance, forming a little tree, then a man, and so on. Each creation exists only for a fleeting moment. Thus, the breaking apart of a chest is no more a tragedy than its initial assembly was a triumph.

24. Carrying an angry expression is unnatural, especially when it persists until death or fades away, never to reignite. This should tell you it's against reason. If the sense of having been wronged disappears, what purpose does continuing in anger serve?

25. Nature, the architect of the universe, continuously transforms all you see, creating new entities from the old, ensuring the world remains perpetually renewed.

26. When wronged, reflect on the beliefs about right and wrong that motivated the offender. Understanding this, you'll find room for pity rather than anger. If you share these beliefs, forgiveness is your only course. If not, you're better positioned to empathize with their mistake.

27. Avoid longing for what you don't have. Instead, appreciate the value of what you do possess, considering how much you'd desire these things if they weren't already yours. But be wary of overvaluing them, lest their loss disturbs you.

28. Find solace within yourself. The rational mind is at peace when it acts justly and fulfills its nature.

. . .

29. Let go of illusions. Stop being pulled in different directions. Focus on the present. Analyze the nature of what happens to you or others, breaking down events to their causes and effects. Contemplate your mortality. Leave grievances where they occurred.

30. Pay attention to the discourse. Immerse your mind in the actions and the actors.

31. Adorn yourself with simplicity, modesty, and indifference to things non-essential to virtue. Embrace humanity. Follow the divine. Remember, as it is often said, "All things are governed by law." This knowledge alone simplifies life's concerns.

32. On death: it leads to dispersal if we are made of atoms; if a single entity, then to extinction or change.

33. On pain: what cannot be endured will end us; what can be endured should be tolerated. The mind can maintain its peace by detaching, and the intellect remains unaffected. Let the parts that suffer speak for themselves, if they can.

34. On fame: consider the values and pursuits of those who seek it. Like sand dunes that bury what was before, the past is quickly obscured by the present.

. . .

35. "To a mind that sees the grandeur of all time and existence, do you think human life appears significant?" "Impossible," he replied. "Then such a person won't find death frightening." "Not in the least."

36. "The true mark of a king is to do good and be criticized for it."

37. It's disgraceful for the face to obey, to conform and beautify itself as the mind dictates, while the mind cannot shape and beautify itself by its own accord.

38. One should not be angered by events, for they are indifferent to our feelings.

39. May you bring joy to the immortal gods and to us.

40. Life, like ripe grain, must to the harvest yield. One exists, another does not.

41. If the gods have overlooked me, and my child as well, there's a reason for it too.

42. For goodness and justice are with me.

·   ·   ·

43. Do not partake in mourning; do not be distressed.

44. "But I would respond justly, saying, 'You are mistaken, sir, if you believe a person of any merit should consider the risk of life and death, and not focus solely on this: whether his actions are just or unjust, those of a good person or a bad one.'"

45. "This is the truth, men of Athens: wherever a man decides to stand, believing it to be right, or wherever he is placed by his leader, there he must stay and confront danger, valuing nothing above the shame of dishonor, not even death."

46. "But consider, my friend, whether true virtue and excellence might be something more than just surviving and ensuring survival. Perhaps a truly courageous man should ignore the obsession with living at all costs, and instead, leaving these concerns to the gods and heeding the women who say that no one can evade their destiny, he should focus on how to live the remaining part of his life as honorably as possible."

47. Imagine yourself tracing the courses of the stars, and constantly reflect on the transformation of elements into one another. Such thoughts cleanse the dirt of terrestrial life.

48. Plato's noble saying is worth noting: when discussing humanity, we should view earthly matters as if from a vantage point above—herds, armies, farmlands, weddings and divorces,

births and deaths, the uproar of courts, secluded places, diverse cultures, celebrations, mourning, markets—a mixture of everything, and an order born of opposites.

49. Reflect on the past, the numerous shifts of empires. You can predict the future, for it will surely follow the same pattern, unable to break away from the rhythm of the present. Thus, examining human life for forty years or ten thousand is the same. What more will you see?

50. And

> What originates from the earth returns to it,
>> And what is born of heavenly essence
>> Ascends back to the stars.

Or could this be the unraveling of atoms and the dispersal of unfeeling elements?

51. And

> With nourishment and enchantments,
>> Deflecting life's course to evade death.
>> . . . .
>> But when life's breath is bestowed by the divine,
>> It is our duty to endure the inevitable struggles without complaint.

52. More arrogant, yet no more sociable, modest, composed in adversity, or forgiving of your neighbors' shortcomings.

53. When a task aligns with the logic shared by gods and humans, no harm should be feared. For when an action is successful and natural, no danger lurks.

54. At all times, it is within your power to gracefully accept your current situation, to treat those around you fairly, and to scrutinize your immediate perceptions to ensure nothing is accepted without due thought.

55. Do not concern yourself with the guiding principles of others; focus instead on where nature guides you—both the universal nature through your experiences, and your own nature through your actions. Each entity must act in accordance with its nature; and all other entities are designed to serve rational beings, just as in any hierarchy, the lesser serves the greater, yet rational beings exist to serve one another.

The essence of being human is to be social; secondly, to resist the sway of physical sensations firmly, for it is the nature of rational and conscious activity to set its own limits and not be overwhelmed by either sensory experiences or impulses—both of which are animalistic. Conscious activity asserts dominance and refuses to be subdued by lesser forces. And rightfully so, for it is uniquely equipped to utilize all others.

The third aspect of rational existence is the avoidance of impulsiveness and falsehood. Thus, let the guiding part of oneself adhere to these principles, and proceed unerringly, for it will have all that it needs.

. . .

56. Live the remainder of your life as though you have been reborn, and from this point forward, live in harmony with nature.

57. Embrace only what fate weaves into your life, for what could be more harmonious?

58. In every situation, remember those who have faced similar events before you, how they reacted with dissatisfaction, bewilderment, and blamed fate. Where are they now? Gone. So why aspire to be like them? Why not leave such misguided responses to those who provoke and are affected by them, and instead focus solely on how you can positively utilize these occurrences? For then you will make good use of them, and they will become material for you to shape. Just be sure to commit to your own excellence in all you do; and remember that the material is neutral, but your actions are not.

59. Look within yourself, for there lies a spring of goodness, always ready to flow if you keep digging.

60. Your body must be steady and composed, whether in motion or at rest, not slack or uncontrolled. Just as the mind maintains a composed and graceful face, it must also govern the whole body. However, ensure this is done naturally, without pretense.

. . .

61. The art of living resembles wrestling more than dancing; it demands readiness and steadfastness to face whatever comes, even the unexpected.

62. Always ponder on the nature of those whose approval you seek, and what drives their thoughts. This understanding will prevent you from blaming those who offend unknowingly, and you will no longer crave their approval once you grasp the roots of their opinions and desires.

63. "EVERY SOUL," it is said, "is deprived of truth unwillingly." The same is true for justice, self-control, kindness, and all such virtues. Remembering this is crucial, as it will make you more compassionate towards everyone.

64. In every instance of pain, remind yourself that there is nothing shameful about it, nor does it deteriorate the mind that governs us, for it does not harm the mind's rational or social abilities. Often, remember Epicurus' advice: that pain is neither endless nor insufferable, as long as you remember its limits and don't exaggerate it in your mind. Also, many discomforts, similar to pain like drowsiness, fever, and loss of appetite, often go unnoticed. When you're upset by any of these, remind yourself that you're succumbing to pain.

65. Be cautious not to adopt the same feelings towards misanthropes as they harbor towards humanity.

· · ·

66. How can we assert that Telauges was of better character than Socrates? It's insufficient to say Socrates died more famously, debated more skillfully, showed greater endurance in the cold, and nobly refused to arrest the Salaminian. (His rumored strut through the streets raises questions, if true.) Instead, we should consider the nature of Socrates' soul. Was he satisfied being just in his interactions and devout towards the gods, not vexed by others' wickedness, nor tolerating ignorance, nor seeing anything as strange or unbearable, nor letting his mind be swayed by bodily sensations?

67. Nature hasn't entangled you so deeply with your surroundings that you can't distinguish and control your own affairs. It's entirely possible to be divine and yet unrecognized. Remember this and that very little is needed for a happy life. Do not despair of attaining freedom, dignity, generosity, and devotion to the divine, even if you lose hope of becoming a philosopher or scientist.

68. To live freely in utmost tranquility, even amidst the chaos of others' opinions or the physical threats to our mortal bodies, is within our reach. For what stops the mind from maintaining its peace, from making true judgments about its surroundings, and from being ready to utilize whatever it encounters? Thus, judgment can confront any situation, recognizing its true nature beyond superficial appearances. Similarly, when something unexpected happens, we can welcome it as exactly what we were looking for. For everything serves as material for practicing rational and civic virtues, embodying the skills of either a human or a divine being. Nothing is too novel or challenging, but rather familiar and manageable.

· · ·

69. The hallmark of a fully developed character is to navigate each day as if it were your last, without anxiety, lethargy, or deceit.

70. The gods, immortal as they are, don't despair over enduring humanity's follies for eons, nor do they cease to care for them. Yet, you, who are fleeting, lose hope—even when you count yourself among the flawed!

71. It's illogical to avoid your own faults, which you can change, while trying to escape others' faults, which you cannot.

72. Anything that the rational and social part of us finds to be neither logical nor communal, it rightly considers beneath itself.

73. When you've done a good deed and someone has benefited from it, why seek a third reward, like fools do, either in the form of recognition or repayment?

74. No one grows tired of receiving kindness. Acting in harmony with nature is a form of kindness. Never tire of receiving or giving it.

75. The nature of the universe intended to create a world of order. Now, either everything happens as a direct result of this

intention, or even the universe's grand designs are without purpose. Keep this in mind; it will bring you peace in many respects.

BOOK 8

1. RECOGNIZING THE VANITY OF FAME HELPS YOU SEE THAT YOU cannot live your entire life, or at least from youth onwards, as a philosopher. It's clear to others, and to yourself, that you are far from the path of philosophy. Corruption has made it difficult for you to earn the reputation of a philosopher, and your current role further complicates this. If you truly understand what matters, then forget about appearances and be satisfied to live out your days, however many, according to your true nature. Focus on what your nature desires, and let nothing else divert you. You've sought happiness in many places—logic, wealth, fame, pleasure—without success. Where then can it be found? In fulfilling the demands of human nature. And how is this achieved? By adhering to principles that guide your desires and actions. What principles? Those that define good and evil, asserting that nothing is good if it does not make us just, temperate, courageous, and free; and nothing is evil if it does not do the opposite.

. . .

2. Before every action, ask yourself: How does this affect me? Will I regret it? Soon, I'll be dead and gone. What more do I seek, if my current work embodies that of an intelligent, social being, on par with God?

3. How do Alexander, Gaius, and Pompey stack up against Diogenes, Heraclitus, and Socrates? The latter delved deep into matters, understanding their causes and materials, guided by the same principles. The former, however, showed immense foresight and were bound by their duties.

4. They will continue doing the same things, even if you're consumed with anger.

5. First, don't be troubled, for everything happens according to the nature of the universe, and soon, you'll be nothing and nowhere, just like Hadrian and Augustus now. Then, examine the issue closely, and, remembering you must be a good person, doing what humanity requires, proceed without hesitation, speaking what you believe is right. But do so with kindness, modesty, and sincerity.

6. The purpose of universal nature is to move things around, to transform them, to lift them up and carry them elsewhere. Everything undergoes change, yet there's no reason to fear anything new. Everything is familiar and equally fleeting.

.   .   .

7. Every nature is satisfied with itself when it follows its path well. A rational nature is on the right path when it accepts nothing false or uncertain in its thoughts, directs its impulses only towards acts of community, limits its desires and aversions to what it can control, and accepts all that is allotted by the universal nature. For it is part of that nature, just as the nature of a leaf is part of a plant's nature—though the leaf is part of a nature without sensation or reason and prone to obstacles, whereas human nature is part of a nature that is free, intelligent, and just, distributing equal shares according to worth in time, substance, cause, activity, and circumstance. But don't weigh whether one thing equals another in every case; consider whether, on the whole, this equals that in total.

8. You may claim you have no time to read. Yet, you have time to check your arrogance; you have time to rise above pleasures and pains; you have time to transcend the desire for fame, and not to be irritated by foolish and ungrateful people—indeed, even to care for them.

9. Let no one hear you complain about life at court again; in fact, let no one hear you complain about your own life at all.

10. Repentance is a form of self-reproach for neglecting something beneficial. Hence, the good must be beneficial, and a truly good person must preserve it. But a truly good person would never regret missing out on a pleasure. Therefore, pleasure is neither beneficial nor good.

.   .   .

11. What is this entity in its essence? What are its substance and material? What is its purpose or nature? What role does it play in the world? How long does it last?

12. When you find it hard to get out of bed, remind yourself that it's your nature and duty as a human to contribute to society, while sleeping is something you share with animals that lack reason. What aligns with a creature's nature is right, innate, and indeed more satisfying for it.

13. Make it a constant practice, whenever possible, to apply the principles of natural science, the understanding of emotions, and logical reasoning.

14. Whenever you encounter someone, quickly consider: "What does this person believe about right and wrong?" If you understand their views on pleasure, pain, fame, disgrace, death, and life, you won't be shocked or find it odd when they behave in certain ways. Remember, they are driven by their beliefs.

15. Keep in mind that it's just as illogical to be surprised by a fig tree producing figs as it is to be taken aback by the natural outcomes of the world. Likewise, it's unreasonable for a doctor to be startled by a fever in a patient or a ship captain by a sudden bad wind.

16. Remember, choosing to change direction and accept correction is also an exercise of free will. Your actions are driven by your own desires and decisions, indeed by your own intellect.

· · ·

17. If it's within your power, why not do it? If it's someone else's responsibility, who are you blaming—mere particles or the gods? Either way, it's pointless. No one is at fault. If possible, guide the one at fault; if not, try to fix the issue; and if that's not possible, what's the point of blame? Nothing should be done without reason.

18. What dies doesn't leave the universe. If it stays, it transforms here and breaks down into its basic elements, which are also parts of the universe and you. These elements change too, without complaint.

19. Everything is made with a purpose in mind—a horse, a grapevine. Why be surprised? Even the sun could say, "I exist for a reason," as could the other gods. So, for what purpose were you created? Surely not merely for pleasure. See if that thought is satisfying.

20. Nature cares just as much for the end of things as for their beginning and continuation, just like someone throwing a ball. What benefit is there in the ball rising, or what harm in it falling or having fallen? What benefit is there in a bubble staying intact, or harm in it popping? The same goes for a lamp.

21. Examine it closely, see what it becomes when aged, sick, or in desire.

Both those who praise and those praised, those who remember and those remembered, are ephemeral. Moreover, all this occurs in a small part of the world, and even here not everyone agrees, and no one is entirely consistent with themselves. And the entire earth is but a speck in the universe.

22. Focus on the essence, the foundational principle, the deed, the meaning.

You are right to endure these challenges. But wouldn't you prefer to be good today rather than hoping to be good tomorrow?

23. What am I doing? I'm doing it for the good of humanity. What happens to me? I leave that to the gods and the source of all things, from which all events are intricately linked.

24. What does bathing mean to you—oil, sweat, grime, greasy water, all things unpleasant? So it is with every aspect of life and every object.

25. Lucilla buried Verus, and then she herself was buried by others. Secunda buried Maximus, and then Secunda was buried. Epitynchanus buried Diotimus, and then was buried himself. Antoninus buried Faustina, and then Antoninus was buried. This is the way of all things. Celer buried Hadrian, and then Celer was buried. Those quick-witted individuals, whether they were seers or simply full of pride, where are they now? Brilliant minds like Charax, Demetrius the Platonist, Eudaemon, and others. All of them fleeting, long since dead. Some were forgotten quickly, while others became legends. Yet, some have even vanished from legends. Remember then, that your body

must either disperse, or your soul must be extinguished or relocated.

26. A man's happiness lies in doing what is proper for a human. It is right for a human to show kindness to their own kind, to overlook the temptations of the senses, to recognize what seems plausible, and to understand the nature of the universe and the events within it comprehensively.

27. There are three relationships: one to the body that houses you; the second to the divine cause from which everything emanates; and the third to those with whom you share your life.

28. Pain is either a bodily affliction—then let the body express its opinion—or it belongs to the soul. But the soul has the power to maintain its peace and not view pain as a misfortune. Every judgment, urge, desire, and aversion originates from within, and nothing external can influence the mind.

29. Erase your false beliefs by reminding yourself: now it is within my power to prevent any evil, desire, or disturbance from entering my soul. By observing everything, I understand its true nature and use each according to its worth. Remember this ability you possess by nature.

30. Speak in the senate and to anyone else, whoever they may be, fittingly and without pretense. Use straightforward language.

· · ·

31. Augustus' court, his wife, daughter, descendants, ancestors, sister, Agrippa, relatives, household, friends, Areius, Maecenas, physicians, and priests—all are gone. Now, look at other records and consider the demise of an entire court, not just one person, like the Pompeii. And on the tombs, it reads—The last of his line. Think about the efforts of those before to leave behind an heir; and yet, inevitably, someone must be the last. Reflect on the extinction of an entire lineage.

32. We must construct our lives action by action, satisfied if each achieves its purpose as best as it can. And nothing can prevent you from doing so.—But external circumstances might interfere. —No external force can stop you from acting with justice, moderation, and thoughtfulness.—But perhaps another endeavor will be obstructed.—In accepting the obstruction and being willing to redirect your efforts to what is permissible, a new opportunity for action presents itself in place of the one obstructed, fitting seamlessly into the life you are crafting.

33. Accept gifts without arrogance and let go without struggle.

34. Imagine seeing a limb—a hand, a foot, or a head—severed from the body, lying apart from the rest. This is the state a person finds themselves in when they reject what occurs or acts against the common good. They sever themselves from nature's unity, despite being born a part of it. However, the beauty lies in our ability to reconnect with this unity. Unlike any other creation, humans have the unique ability to rejoin the whole after separation, a privilege granted by God. He has not only

made it possible for us never to be torn from this unity but also to return and reintegrate, should we choose to detach.

35. Just as we have been endowed with various abilities by the nature of rational beings, so too have we received the power to transform obstacles into opportunities, integrating them into our destined path, just as nature does.

36. Do not be overwhelmed by the entirety of your life, nor dwell on past troubles or future worries. Instead, confront each immediate challenge by asking, "What here is truly insurmountable?" You'll find it hard to admit anything is. Remember, it's neither the past nor the future that troubles you, but always the present—and the present can be managed if you isolate it and reprimand your mind for not withstanding what is essentially a minor issue.

37. Are Pantheia or Pergamos mourning by Verus's coffin? Or Chabrias or Diotimus by Hadrian's? Absurd! Even if they were, would the deceased notice? And if they noticed, would it bring them joy? And if it did, would that grant them immortality? They were destined to age and then to die. What then is the point of such mourning? All that remains is decay and the illusion of significance.

38. "OBSERVE KEENLY AND JUDGE WISELY," advises the philosopher.

. . .

39. Within the nature of a rational being, I find no virtue in conflict with justice, but I see self-control as the adversary of pleasure.

40. If you dismiss your perception of something as painful, you become immune to suffering. "What do you mean by 'you'?" Your reasoning. "But I am not just my reasoning." Let that be. Regardless, let your reasoning be untroubled. Should another part of you suffer, let it assess the situation independently.

41. An obstacle to perception is detrimental to an animal's nature, just as an obstacle to impulse is. Similarly, for plants, any hindrance is harmful to their nature. Thus, an impediment to intelligence is a misfortune for a being of reason. Apply this understanding to yourself. Are you affected by pain or pleasure? Leave that to the senses. Faced with an obstacle to your desires? If you acted without considering the usual constraints, then it's a setback. However, if you acknowledge these universal limitations, you've neither been harmed nor truly obstructed. Nothing external can interfere with the operations of the mind, which, when fully autonomous and self-sufficient, is like "a sphere in solitary rotation."

42. I am unworthy of causing myself distress, for I have never intentionally caused distress to another.

43. Different things delight different people. For me, delight comes from possessing a sound mind—one that welcomes every

person and every occurrence with kindness, sees the value in everything, and uses each thing according to its worth.

44. Give yourself this moment. Those who pursue fame don't realize that future generations will resemble those they currently find burdensome—and they, too, will be mortal. Why should it matter to you if future voices echo such opinions about you?

45. Place me wherever you wish; there too, my divine spirit will be gracious—that is, content if it can feel and act according to its nature.

Is it worth it, to allow my soul to deteriorate into a state worse than its natural one, becoming groveling, lustful, cowering, frightened? What is worth that cost?

46. Nothing can happen to a man that isn't a human misfortune, to an ox that isn't in the nature of an ox, to a vine that isn't in the nature of a vine, or to a stone that isn't proper to a stone. If then what is usual and natural happens to each, why complain? Common nature brings nothing unbearable.

47. If an external thing causes you pain, it's not the thing itself but your judgment of it that disturbs you. And you have the power to erase this judgment now. If something within your own disposition pains you, what stops you from changing your opinion? And if you're pained because you're not doing something you believe is right, why not act instead of complain? If an insurmountable obstacle is in the way, don't be grieved, for its not

being done isn't up to you. If you believe life isn't worth living if this can't be done, then leave life contentedly, just like someone who dies actively engaged and satisfied despite obstacles.

48. Remember that the ruling faculty is invincible when it is focused and satisfied with itself, not acting against its will, even if it resists out of sheer stubbornness. What then when it makes a judgment aided by reason and deliberate choice? Thus, a mind free from passions is a fortress, for there is nothing more secure for a man to retreat to and be safe. Those who haven't realized this are ignorant; those who have but don't seek refuge are unhappy.

49. Limit yourself to what initial impressions report. For example, if it's reported that someone speaks ill of you, that's all that's reported; not that you've been harmed. If I see my child is sick, that's what I see; but not that he's in danger. Stick to initial impressions and add nothing more from within; then, nothing can harm you. Or rather, add something like someone who understands everything that happens in the world.

50. A bitter cucumber? Leave it be. Brambles in your way? Simply walk around them. That's all there is to it; there's no need to question, "Why do such things exist in the world?" A naturalist would find such questioning laughable, just as a carpenter or cobbler would chuckle if you complained about the shavings and scraps in their workshop. They have a place to discard them, but the universe has nowhere outside itself. Its marvel lies in its self-containment, turning everything that decays, ages, or becomes obsolete back into itself, creating anew

from these very elements. It requires no external materials or a dumping ground for waste. It is self-sufficient, using its own space, materials, and craftsmanship.

51. Do not be careless in your actions, confused in your speech, or distracted in your thoughts. Do not let your soul become either completely consumed or agitated, nor be overly busy in life. People may harm, tear apart, and curse. How, then, can you maintain a pure, sound, sober, and fair mind? It's like standing next to a clear, sweet spring and cursing it, yet it continues to provide drinkable water. If you throw mud or dung into it, the spring quickly disperses and cleanses them, remaining pure. How can you maintain a perpetual fountain within you, not just a temporary well? By constantly guarding your freedom with kindness, simplicity, and modesty.

52. Someone who does not understand what the universe is, does not know where they are. Someone who does not grasp the purpose of nature, does not know who they are or what the universe is. Failing in these understandings, one cannot even comprehend their own purpose. What, then, to make of someone who seeks or avoids the applause of those who themselves are lost, not knowing where they are or who they are?

53. Why seek praise from someone who curses themselves every hour? Why try to please someone who cannot find pleasure in themselves? Can a person who regrets nearly everything they do truly be content with themselves?

. . .

54. Do not merely breathe the air around you, but also think with the intelligence that permeates everything. This intelligent force is as widespread and fills those open to it, just as air fills those who breathe.

55. On a grand scale, wickedness does not harm the universe, and on a personal level, it does not harm others. It only harms the one who harbors it, and they can choose to rid themselves of it whenever they wish.

56. To my ability to choose, my neighbor's choices are as irrelevant as their breath and body. Although we were created for one another, our decision-making powers are sovereign. Otherwise, my neighbor's misdeeds would harm me, which is not the divine intention, so that no one else can dictate my misfortune.

57. The sun seems to pour its radiance everywhere, yet it is never diminished. This outpouring is a form of tension; its beams, known as "rays," stretch out in every direction. Consider a beam of sunlight entering a dark room through a small opening. It extends straight, as if pushing against any solid object in its path, resting there without falling or slipping away. Similarly, the mind should radiate without draining itself, maintaining its strength even when faced with obstacles, illuminating what allows its light to pass through. Anything that blocks the ray simply deprives itself of light.

· · ·

58. Fear of death boils down to either fearing the loss of sensation or fearing a transformation to a different state of existence. If it's the loss of sensation, then there's no evil to experience; if it's a transformation, you'll simply become a different kind of living being, continuing to exist.

59. Humans exist for the sake of one another. Teach them or tolerate them.

60. Unlike an arrow, the mind's progress, even when cautious or contemplative, remains directed towards its goal.

61. Understand the perspective of others and let them understand yours.

BOOK 9

1. ACTING UNJUSTLY IS AN ACT OF IMPIETY. NATURE DESIGNED rational beings to help each other, to provide mutual aid, and never to harm. Those who go against this design offend against the most ancient gods. Liars are also impious, for Nature represents things as they truly are, linking all realities to the totality of existence. She embodies Truth and is the source of all truths.

The deliberate liar commits an impiety by harming another through deception, while the unintentional liar clashes with Nature's reality, creating disharmony. Those who are not in accordance with reality are at war with themselves, having ignored Nature's guidance to distinguish truth from falsehood. Additionally, seeing pleasures as goods and pains as evils is impious, leading one to unjustly criticize Nature for what he sees as unfair distributions of pleasure and hardship.

Fearing hardship, or inevitable cosmic events, is also impious. The pursuit of pleasure at any cost leads to injustice, another form of impiety. We should remain neutral towards things Nature treats impartially, as she would not have created them otherwise. Thus, viewing labor and pleasure, life and death, fame and obscurity with anything but neutrality is to act impiously.

By "equal use," I mean their impartial occurrence, following a sequence of events set in motion by Providence from the beginning, establishing principles and generative powers for the creation of substances, changes, and sequences.

2. It would have been more dignified to leave this world untouched by lies, hypocrisy, excess, and arrogance. Yet, if you find yourself indulging in these vices until your final breath, consider it the next best option. Or perhaps you're still entangled in wrongdoing, unconvinced by your experiences to escape this metaphorical plague? For a corrupted mind is a far more devastating affliction than any physical disease or environmental change. The latter affects animals in their physical existence; the former undermines humans in their essence.

3. Do not scorn death but welcome it, as it is also a desire of nature. Just as it is natural to age, to grow and mature, to develop physically and undergo the various stages of life, so too is it natural to pass away. Embracing death with reason means awaiting it not with hatred or pride but as a natural part of life. And as you look forward to the birth of a child with anticipation, similarly, await the moment your soul frees itself from its mortal coil.

If you're looking for a guiding principle to make peace with death, consider this: reflect on what you're leaving behind and the type of people you'll no longer have to deal with. Don't harbor resentment towards them, but show compassion and patience, all the while remembering you're leaving behind those who don't share your values. The possibility of living with like-minded individuals might be the only thing that could make us cling to life. But the reality of constant discord makes us welcome death, so we don't lose ourselves in the fray.

4. Those who sin, do so against themselves; those who are unjust, wrong themselves by becoming corrupt.

5. Often, injustice comes from inaction, not just from harmful actions.

6. The current belief that understands truth, the action that benefits the common good, and the mindset that accepts everything external as it happens—these are enough.

7. Eliminate fantasies; control impulses; suppress desires; keep your intellect in check.

8. In irrational animals, life is shared collectively; in rational beings, an intellectual soul is distributed among individuals. Similarly, there is one earth for all earthly beings, one light by which we see, and one air we all breathe—everything that lives and sees.

9. All things gravitate towards their own kind. Earthly elements descend; liquids merge; air combines unless forcefully separated; fire rises, eager to unite with any spark here below, for it ignites more readily when less diluted by non-combustible

elements. Thus, beings with a common intellect are drawn even more towards their kin. The higher their nature, the more inclined they are to connect and blend with their own kind.

Among irrational animals, we observe social structures, familial bonds, and a form of affection. Here, a unifying force operates at a higher level, though not in plants or inanimate objects. But among rational beings, we see communities, friendships, families, gatherings, agreements, and even peace in conflict. And in higher realms, despite separation, there exists a unity, like among the stars. The climb towards a superior form fosters a connection even among the disparate.

Observe the present situation. Only intellectual beings have forgotten their natural affinity and cohesion. Here alone, the unifying force is invisible. Yet, despite their attempts to isolate, they remain interconnected, for nature always prevails. Upon closer inspection, it's easier to find an earthly element separated from its kind than a person isolated from humanity.

10. Both humans and gods, along with the cosmos, bear fruit; each in its own season. Though the term is commonly associated with vines and similar plants, this is inconsequential. Reason too bears its fruit, both universally and individually, and from reason emerge other entities, sharing its essence.

11. If possible, enlighten them; if not, remember that you've been granted kindness for this very reason. The gods extend their kindness to such individuals, even aiding them in achieving health, wealth, and renown. This is their benevolence. And you are allowed the same. Or tell me, who stands in your way?

· · ·

12. Work, but not with misery or in search of pity or admiration; instead, aspire to only one thing: to act or rest as dictated by communal logic.

13. Today, I evaded all troubles, or rather, I expelled them, for they were not external but within my own perception.

14. All experiences are familiar, fleeting, and base in nature. Everything now is as it was in the times of those we have laid to rest.

15. Things exist independently, without self-awareness or judgment. What then passes judgment on them? Our guiding principle.

16. For a rational, social being, good and evil reside not in feelings but in actions, just as virtue and vice are determined by deeds, not emotions.

17. For a stone launched into the air, descending is no misfortune, just as being thrown is not a blessing.

18. Look into their minds, and you'll see the judges you fear and how they critique themselves.

. . .

19. Everything is undergoing change. You are perpetually transforming and, in a way, deteriorating, as is the entire universe.

20. Leave another's misdeeds to them.

21. The end of an endeavor, the suppression of impulses and opinions, and a type of demise—none of these are misfortunes. Reflect on your life's phases—childhood, adolescence, young adulthood, and later years: each transition resembles a form of death. Is there anything here to dread? Consider your life under your grandfather, then your mother, then your father. Upon discovering numerous other shifts and endings, contemplate: was there anything to fear? Therefore, the cessation, suppression, and alteration of your entire life should not be feared.

22. Rush towards your own intellect, that of the universe, and that of the individual in question. To your own, to ensure it acts fairly; to that of the universe, to recall the part you play in it; to that of the individual, to discern whether they act out of ignorance or wisdom, while recognizing their kinship to you.

23. Just as you are an integral part of a community, let every one of your actions contribute to communal life. Any act that does not serve this communal purpose fragments your life, preventing unity, and is divisive, akin to a citizen who isolates himself from the collective harmony.

. . .

24. The tantrums and games of children, likened to "little spirits carrying corpses," vividly illustrate the Underworld's imagery[1].

25. Assess the essence of the cause, stripping away its material aspects, and then observe it. Also, determine the duration—how long this particular essence is naturally inclined to exist.

26. You have faced countless troubles because you were not satisfied with your guiding reason performing its inherent function. But let's leave that behind.

27. When someone criticizes, despises, or speaks against you, delve into their minds, see what kind of people they are. You'll realize there's no need to stress over their opinions of you. Yet, you must show them kindness, for they are naturally our allies. The gods also support them in various ways—through dreams, through oracles—towards resolving the very issues they grapple with.

28. The cycles of the universe are constant, fluctuating from one era to the next. Either the universal mind initiates movement for each individual entity—if so, embrace this movement—or it initiated a singular motion, leading to subsequent events as a consequence. (Think of atoms or indivisibles.) If the universe is divine, all is well; if it's random, don't let yourself be ruled by randomness.

Soon we'll all be buried by the earth. Then the earth will transform, and the products of this transformation will continue evolving indefinitely. Reflecting on the rapid waves of change and alteration, one will find mortal concerns trivial.

29. The universal substance is akin to a raging winter stream: it sweeps everything away. How insignificant are these political matters and the so-called pragmatically philosophical individuals—mere trifles. What to do, then? Fulfill what nature demands of you now. Proceed if you can, and don't concern yourself with recognition. Don't yearn for Plato's Republic; be satisfied with any progress, however minor, and regard its result as significant. Who will change their beliefs? Without such changes, what exists besides the pretense of obedience by those in agony? Forget Alexander, Philip, and Demetrius of Phalerum. Let them judge if they aligned with what the universal nature intended and adjusted accordingly. If they merely played parts in a tragedy, no one has sentenced me to follow suit. Philosophy's task is straightforward and humble. Do not draw me into ostentation.

30. From above, gaze upon the myriad throngs of people, diverse rituals, and all types of journeys through storms and calm. Reflect on the variations in being born, living together, and dying. Think about the lives of those in ancient times, those yet to come, and those currently living in remote regions; consider how many are unaware of your name, how many will soon forget it, how many who now perhaps commend you will quickly criticize you. Realize that neither memory, fame, nor any other pursuit truly matters.

· · ·

31. Peace comes from accepting the things beyond our control and justice from our own actions—specifically, our intentions and actions aimed at the common good, aligning with our true nature.

32. You can free yourself from many unnecessary worries that exist solely in your imagination. By embracing the vastness of the universe in your mind, pondering the endless expanse of time, and reflecting on the swift change of each thing—from its inception to its end—you'll find ample space for yourself. Consider how brief the span from birth to death is, how vast the era before birth, and equally infinite the time after death.

33. Everything you see will soon vanish, and those who witness this vanishing will also disappear. Even those who live the longest won't have a different fate in death than those who die young.

34. Reflect on the essence of their thoughts, their pursuits, and their aversions. Consider their souls laid bare. When they think their criticism or praise affects you, it's merely an illusion!

35. Loss is simply a form of change, which the nature of the universe delights in. Everything happens in accordance with this principle. Similar events have occurred since the dawn of time and will continue indefinitely. So, why assert that things have always and will always turn for the worse, as if no divine power could ever rectify matters, condemning the world to perpetual misfortune?

· · ·

36. Consider the decay inherent in all things: water, dust, bones, decay. Or again: marble is just solidified soil, gold and silver mere sediments, clothing is animal fur, purple dye is blood, and so on. Even our breath is transient, constantly changing.

37. Enough of this wretched existence, enough of the complaints and mimicry! Why are you distressed? What's new here? What unsettles you—is it the cause? Examine it. Or is it the matter at hand? Then scrutinize that. Beyond these, there's nothing. Now, it's time to become more sincere and gracious towards the divine.

Whether you ponder these things for a century or just three years makes no difference.

38. If he did wrong, thc harm is his own. But it's possible he did no wrong.

39. Either everything originates from a single intelligent source, forming a unified whole where the part shouldn't lament what benefits the whole; or we're merely a mix of atoms, with nothing but mingling and separation. So, why distress yourself? Tell your ruling faculty: "You're dead, you've fallen, you've turned into a beast; you're merely acting, herding, surviving."

40. Either the gods are powerless, or they wield power. If powerless, why pray to them? If powerful, why not pray for freedom from fear, desire, and sorrow, rather than for specific

outcomes? If they can aid us, surely they can help in these matters. Maybe you believe the gods have left these things up to us. Then, isn't it better to use what's within our control freely, rather than fret over what's beyond our reach? And who said the gods don't help with things within our control? Shift your prayers: Instead of "How can I sleep with them?" ask "How can I stop desiring them?" Instead of "How can I get rid of them?" ask "How can I stop wishing them gone?" Instead of "How can I prevent losing my child?" ask "How can I not fear losing them?" Transform your prayers in this way and observe the outcome.

41. Epicurus stated, "During my illness, I did not dwell on my physical discomforts when speaking with visitors. Instead, I engaged in discussions on the core principles of natural philosophy, focusing on how the mind can maintain tranquility and uphold its well-being amidst bodily disturbances. I didn't allow physicians to boast as though they were performing some grand act; my life continued pleasantly and well." He advises us to follow his example in times of sickness or adversity. Never forsake philosophy, regardless of the hardships you encounter, and avoid pointless discussions with those who lack understanding of nature—a principle embraced by all philosophical schools. Focus solely on the task at hand and the means by which you accomplish it.

42. When confronted with someone's shamelessness, immediately ask yourself: "Is it possible for shameless people not to exist?" It's not. Therefore, expecting the impossible is futile. This person is simply one of the many shameless individuals that inevitably exist in the world. Keep this realization in mind for dealing with deceivers, traitors, and all kinds of wrong-

doers. Remembering that such people must exist helps you view them more compassionately.

It's also beneficial to quickly reflect on the virtues nature has endowed us with to counteract any wrongdoing. For instance, gentleness is given as a remedy for harshness, and similarly, other virtues are provided to counteract other faults. It's within your power to guide those who have erred, as every wrongdoer has merely lost their way. And ask yourself, how have you been harmed? You'll discover that no one who offends you can diminish your mind.

The true source of evil and harm lies within your own mind. Why be surprised when an ignorant person acts ignorantly? Consider whether the fault lies with you for not anticipating their error. You had the rational capacity to foresee this mistake, yet you overlooked it and now marvel that they erred.

Especially when feeling aggrieved by disloyalty or ingratitude, reflect on your own actions. The fault lies with you, whether you misplaced your trust in someone's character or failed to give a favor freely, without expecting anything in return. What more could you want after doing a good deed? Isn't the act of kindness itself sufficient? Just as the eye sees and the feet walk without expecting a reward, so too should you do good naturally, contributing to the common good and fulfilling your purpose.

BOOK 10

1. Can you ever be pure, simple, whole, and unadorned, more visible than the body that surrounds you? Will you ever embrace a loving and gentle disposition? Can you ever be complete, lacking nothing, desiring nothing—whether living or lifeless—for pleasure? Not even longing for more time to extend your joy, nor a different place, a different country, or a more pleasant climate? Not even yearning for the company of others? Will you be content with your current situation, finding joy in what you have now, believing that you've received everything from the divine, that all is well with you and will continue to be well, whatever they decide, and whatever they provide to maintain the perfect being—good, just, and beautiful, the creator, supporter, and encompasser of all things, which are dissolved only to be reborn in likeness? Will you live in such harmony with gods and humans, without criticizing them or being judged by them?

2. Consider what your nature demands, as if you were guided solely by it. Then do it and welcome it, provided it does not

degrade your nature as a living being. Next, consider what your nature as a living being calls for. And embrace this too, provided it does not diminish your nature as a rational being. And being rational is also being social. Follow these principles, and let nothing else disturb you.

3. Everything that happens is either bearable or not. If it's bearable, then bear it and stop complaining. If it's unbearable, then stop complaining as well. Your demise will bring it to an end. Just remember: you can bear anything that your mind deems bearable, by deciding it's in your interest or in your nature to do so.

4. If someone is mistaken, kindly instruct them and show them their error. But if you can't, blame yourself, or perhaps not even yourself.

5. Whatever happens to you was destined from the beginning of time. The threads of fate have intertwined your existence with the events that befall you.

6. Whether the universe is a collection of atoms or nature is a system, establish this first: I am part of the whole governed by nature; next, I have a close connection with other similar parts. With this in mind, since I am a part, I shall be content with everything allotted to me by the whole; for nothing is harmful to the part if it benefits the whole. The whole contains nothing detrimental to itself; and while all natures share this principle, the nature of the universe has an additional quality: it cannot be

forced by any external power to produce anything harmful to itself.

By remembering that I am part of such a whole, I shall be content with everything that occurs. And since I am closely related to parts of the same nature as myself, I shall act not against our common interests but always towards them, steering my actions towards the common good and away from the opposite. If this is done, life must flow smoothly, just as the life of a citizen flourishes when he acts for the benefit of his fellow citizens and is satisfied with whatever role the state assigns him.

7. The components of the universe, naturally part of the whole, are destined to transform and eventually perish. This transformation should not be viewed as a misfortune, for if it were, it would imply that the universe is poorly managed, given its parts are designed for change and ultimate dissolution. It's illogical to think that nature would intentionally inflict harm on its components, making them vulnerable to destruction, or that such events occur without nature's awareness. Both notions are far-fetched.

To argue that these transformations are natural, yet react with surprise or displeasure as if they were unnatural, is contradictory. This is especially true when considering that everything dissolves back into the elements from which it was made. This could mean either a dispersal of the elements it was formed from or a conversion of the solid to earth and the ethereal to air, allowing them to be reintegrated into the universe's logic, whether through periodic consumption by fire or constant renewal.

And remember, the solid and the ethereal parts of you are not those you were born with; they are the result of recent nourishment and the air you've breathed. Therefore, it's the acquired, not the innate, that changes—not what you received at birth.

8. Having adopted the titles of good, modest, true, prudent, harmonious, and magnanimous, ensure you live up to them. If you stray, promptly return to these virtues. Remember, being "prudent" means giving careful attention to each matter and remaining impartial; "harmonious" means accepting what the universe assigns you; "magnanimous" means elevating your mind above bodily sensations, fame, death, and all else.

If you embody these virtues without seeking recognition from others, you'll transform and embark on a new life. Clinging to your past self, marred by turmoil, is foolish, like a gladiator who, despite grievous wounds, begs for survival only to face the same fate again.

Embrace these few virtues; if you can maintain them, consider yourself blessed. If you find yourself faltering, retreat to a place where you can stand firm; or, if necessary, leave life not with resentment but simply, freely, modestly, having achieved the dignity of a well-timed departure.

Remembering these virtues is easier when you consider the gods, who favor not flattery but the aspiration for all rational beings to emulate their virtues. Just as the fig tree, dog, bee, and every creature fulfills its nature, so should a human being perform their own unique role.

9. Mimicry, war, terror, paralysis, slavery; day by day, those sacred principles you imagine and dismiss without genuine inquiry will be erased. One must perceive and act in such a way that practical action is accomplished, theoretical study is activated, and the self-assurance derived from understanding each

thing is preserved—hidden, but not concealed. When will you embrace simplicity? When solemnity? When will you recognize the true nature of each thing, its place in the universe, its natural lifespan, its composition, to whom it can belong, and who can give and take it away?

10. A spider takes pride in catching a fly, another in snaring a hare, another in netting a small fish, another in capturing pigs, another bears, another Sarmatians. Are they not all brigands, if you examine their principles?

11. Develop a systematic method for observing how all things transform into one another; focus on this continuously and train yourself in it, for nothing cultivates such greatness of mind. One has shed the body and, realizing that he must soon depart from humanity and leave all these things behind, has devoted himself entirely to justice in his own actions and to the universal nature in all that happens. He does not even consider what others will say, think, or do against him. He is content with only two things: to act justly in the present moment and to love what is now allotted to him. He has dismissed all haste and commotion, desiring nothing other than to traverse the straight path through the law and, by following this path, to follow God.

12. What need is there for suspicion when you can clearly see what ought to be done? If the way forward is clear, proceed with kindness and unwavering resolve. If the path is obscured, pause and seek the best counsel. If other obstacles oppose this course, advance according to your present resources, holding fast to what appears just. To attain this is best, for failure is simply to

stray from this path. One who follows reason in all things is simultaneously relaxed and energetic, both cheerful and steady.

13. Upon waking, ask yourself: Will it make any difference to you if others criticize what is just and noble in you? It will make no difference. Have you forgotten the nature of those who make such a fuss in their praise and blame of others—what they are like in bed, at the table, what they do, what they avoid, what they pursue, what they steal, what they rob, not with hands and feet, but with their most precious part, by which, whenever one wishes, one produces trust, modesty, truth, law, and a good guardian spirit?

14. To nature, which gives and takes back all, the educated and modest man says: "Give what you will; take back what you will." And he says this not defiantly, but obediently and with goodwill toward her.

15. Our time is short. Live as though you were atop a mountain. It doesn't matter whether you're here or there; wherever you are in the world, act as a citizen of a grand city-state. Let others see a true human being living in harmony with nature. If they can't stand it, let them kill you, for that's better than living against your principles.

16. Stop talking about what makes a good person; be one.

· · ·

17. Always think about the entirety of time and the vast expanse of the universe, realizing that all things within it are as minor as a grain of millet, and each moment is as brief as the turn of a screw.

18. Recognize that everything you encounter is already changing, breaking down, and scattering, for nature destines all things to perish.

19. Reflect on how people behave when they eat, sleep, have sex, relieve themselves, and other vulgar activities. Then, consider how they act when in power, filled with arrogance, or lecturing from a high horse. Not long ago, they were under the control of many masters and desires, and they'll be in that position again soon.

20. The universal nature gives each thing what it needs, at the perfect time.

21. "The earth welcomes the rain, and the majestic sky loves (the earth)." The universe rejoices in creating what must be. So, I tell the universe, "I love as you love." Isn't it also said, "This loves to happen"?

22. You have three choices: stay and adapt, leave if you desire, or die having done your duty. That's all there is. So, be happy.

.   .   .

23. Always remember that a meadow is no different from any other place, and everything here is the same as on a mountain peak, a seashore, or anywhere else. You'll find truth in Plato's words: "fencing in a sheepfold on a mountain and milking goats or sheep."

24. What does my guiding faculty mean to me now, and how am I using it? For what purpose do I direct it? Is it irrational? Has it become detached from human connection? Is it so entangled with the body that they move as one?

25. One who runs from his master is a runaway slave. The law is our master, and anyone who breaks the law is a runaway. Those who are distressed, angry, or afraid don't accept what has, is, or will happen—events decreed by the one who rules everything, the law that gives each what is appropriate. Therefore, those who feel fear, grief, or anger are runaways.

26. A man plants his seed in a womb and leaves, then another force takes over, working to develop the child. It's amazing what comes from such a simple start! The baby swallows food, and another force steps in, creating perception, impulse, life, strength, and more. Look at the things produced in such a hidden way, and recognize this power, just as we understand the forces of gravity and buoyancy not with our eyes, but with clear insight.

27. Reflect on the idea that everything happening now has happened before and will happen again. Visualize entire histor-

ical scenes, such as the courts of Hadrian, Antoninus, Philip, Alexander, and Croesus, recognizing that today's events are merely reruns with different actors.

28. Consider anyone upset or dissatisfied as akin to a pig that resists and cries out when being sacrificed. Similarly, a person who laments alone in bed over life's constraints is no different. Remember, only humans have the privilege to willingly accept what happens; for everything else, acceptance is not a choice but a necessity.

29. Before acting, ask yourself, "Would it really matter if death prevented me from doing this?"

30. When someone's mistake offends you, examine your own faults, especially those involving desires for money, pleasure, or fame. This reflection will help you overcome your anger, realizing that the person had little choice in their actions. If possible, help them overcome these compulsions.

31. When you encounter certain people, let them remind you of others, and when you consider yourself, think of the Caesars. Reflect on where all these individuals are now—gone, forgotten. This realization underscores the transience of human affairs. Why not live harmoniously during your brief existence, instead of avoiding opportunities for growth? Everything in life is an exercise for the mind, turning challenges into fuel, much like fire transforms everything thrown into it into light and warmth.

· · ·

32. Never allow anyone to truthfully accuse you of being insincere or unkind; anyone who does is mistaken. Being good and sincere is within your control. Decide to live only if you can be such a person, for reason dictates that life is not worth living otherwise.

33. Ask yourself what the most virtuous action or statement is that you can make right now, and realize it's within your power to do so. Stop making excuses. Embrace the notion that acting in accordance with human nature should be as pleasurable as indulgence is to the hedonist. Unlike physical objects, which are limited by external obstacles, your mind can navigate through any barrier in alignment with its nature. Recognize the ease with which reason can overcome challenges, just as fire rises or a stone falls. Understand that obstacles only affect the body or are perceived through opinion; they cannot truly harm unless allowed by the individual. Remember, no one can harm you but yourself, and adversity can make you stronger if faced with the right mindset. Finally, remember that nothing that doesn't harm the law harms the state or its citizens.

34. For those who embrace true principles, even the simplest phrases can serve as powerful reminders of liberation from grief and fear. Consider the saying, "As the wind scatters leaves on the ground, so too are the generations of men." Your children are like leaves, as are those who praise you loudly or, conversely, those who curse or silently mock. Even those who will celebrate your legacy are no different. These events unfold "in the season of spring," only for the wind to sweep them away. Soon, the forest will produce new leaves to take their place. Yet, everything is transient. Despite this, you chase or avoid things as if they

were everlasting. Before long, you will close your eyes for the last time; and soon after, another will mourn the one who buried you.

35. A healthy eye should be able to see everything within its view without saying, "I want to see only green," as that would indicate a problem. Similarly, healthy ears and a healthy nose should be open to all sounds and scents. A healthy stomach should accept any food, just as a mill grinds whatever it is given. Likewise, a healthy mind should be prepared for anything that might happen. A mind that wishes only for the safety of its children or for universal acclaim is as flawed as an eye that sees only green, or teeth that can chew only soft foods.

36. No one is so beloved that there won't be someone by his deathbed relieved at his passing. Imagine he was virtuous and wise; there will still be someone thinking, "Finally, I am free from that moral overseer. He never criticized us openly, but I always felt judged." That's the fate of a virtuous person. For us, there are countless reasons someone might be glad to see us go. Reflect on this as you approach death, and you'll leave this life more peacefully, thinking, "I am leaving a world where even those I worked hard for, prayed for, and cared about are perhaps relieved at my departure, hoping to benefit from it." Why then should we cling to life here any longer? Yet, leave not with bitterness, but with kindness, generosity, and grace. Do not wrench yourself away, but depart as if death were gently separating soul from body. Nature joined you to these people, and now she's unbinding that connection. You are being released, not from enemies, but as if from family, not with resistance but willingly, for this too is part of nature's course.

· · ·

37. Make it a practice to question, as much as possible with each action, "What is the intention behind this?" Start with yourself, scrutinizing your motives first.

38. Remember, it's the unseen force within us that truly drives our actions: the source of our speech, our life, indeed, our very essence. Never mistake it for the physical body and its organs, which are mere tools, unique only because they grow with us. Without the driving force behind them, these parts are as useless as a weaver's shuttle, a writer's pen, or a driver's whip.

BOOK 11

I. The rational soul possesses unique faculties: self-awareness, introspection, autonomy, the ability to enjoy its own achievements (unlike plants and animals, whose fruits are harvested by others), and the pursuit of its own purpose, regardless of life's duration. Unlike the arts of dance or acting, which are incomplete if interrupted, the soul can achieve fulfillment at any point, declaring, "I possess what is truly mine."

Furthermore, the soul explores the entire universe, the emptiness around it, its own nature, and delves into the endless expanse of time. It understands the cyclical renewal of all existence, recognizing that future generations will witness nothing new, just as past generations have seen everything that exists, due to their inherent similarity. A person of forty years, if wise, has essentially experienced all that has been and will be. The rational soul also embraces neighborly love, dedication to truth and modesty, and places no value higher than itself, mirroring the essence of Law. Therefore, the principle of right reason is indistinguishable from the principle of justice.

. . .

2. The allure of melodious songs, dances, and the pancratium[1] diminishes when you analyze the components, questioning the power of each individual note, movement, or technique, asking, "Is this truly captivating?" This reflection leads to a realization of their insignificance. By applying this method of dissection to everything but virtue and its derivatives, you learn to view them with disdain. This approach should also be applied to life as a whole.

3. Consider the soul that stands ready to depart from the body at any moment, prepared for extinction, dispersal, or continued existence. This readiness stems from personal conviction, not stubbornness as seen in Christians, but from thoughtful and dignified contemplation, capable of convincing others without resorting to dramatics.

4. "I have contributed to the common good; thus, I have served my own interests." Keep this conviction at hand, and persist in such benevolent actions.

5. What is your craft? To excel in goodness, achieved through philosophical teachings on the cosmos's nature and the ideal state of humanity.

6. Tragedy was introduced to reflect our life experiences, to remind us that such events are natural, and to teach us not to be overwhelmed by situations that entertain us in plays. It reassures us that we must endure what is destined, as even those

lamenting "O Cithaeron!" must accept their fate. Poets offer valuable insights, including:

> "If I and my two children have been overlooked by the gods,
>   There is a reason for this too."

And also:

> "We should not be angry at circumstances."

And:

> "Life, like ripe grain, must to the harvest yield."

Such sentiments are noteworthy.

Following tragedy, old comedy emerged, celebrated for its bold freedom of speech and its effectiveness in cautioning against arrogance, a lesson even Diogenes[2] embraced from these works.

Reflect on the purpose of Middle Comedy and the subsequent evolution into New Comedy, which ultimately devolved into mere imitation. Despite this, it's acknowledged that these genres occasionally convey meaningful messages. However, the overarching goal of such poetry and dramaturgy merits contemplation.

7. It strikes me vividly that there is no better state for practicing philosophy than the one you currently find yourself in!

8. A branch severed from its neighbor inevitably becomes detached from the entire tree. Similarly, a person who distances

themselves from just one other individual is essentially disconnecting from the entire community. Unlike a branch, which is cut by external forces, individuals isolate themselves through animosity and avoidance, not realizing they've cut themselves off from society at large.

Yet, we're endowed with a remarkable ability by Zeus, the founder of our community: the power to reconcile with our neighbor and reintegrate into the collective. However, if separation becomes habitual, rejoining becomes increasingly challenging, and the bond may never fully recover. As gardeners observe, a branch that remains attached from the start, sharing in the tree's life force, is fundamentally different from one that's been cut and grafted back on.

Unity in community doesn't require unanimity of thought.

9. Those who resist you as you follow the path of reason won't deter you from right action; similarly, don't let them diminish your goodwill towards them. Protect yourself equally against both losing your temper and abandoning your principles. Anger, just like capitulation, indicates a failure to stand firm. Both are deserters: one through retreat, the other through estrangement from their inherent ally and friend.

10. "Nature is not inferior to art," since art seeks to emulate nature. If this holds true, then the most complete and supreme nature cannot be outdone by artistic endeavor. All arts aim to serve the superior through the creation of the inferior; thus, the same applies to the natural world.

This principle underlies justice, which, in turn, gives rise to other virtues. Justice is compromised when we overvalue trivial matters or when we're easily misled, careless, and inconsistent.

.   .   .

11. The things you chase or flee don't move towards you; rather, you approach them. Stay your judgment, and they too will stand still, leaving you neither in pursuit nor in avoidance.

12. The soul is truly spherical when it neither reaches out for external things nor withdraws into itself, neither swells nor contracts, but shines in the light that reveals both the truth of the world and its own inner truth.

13. If someone despises me, that's their concern. My responsibility is to ensure I don't act or speak in a way that warrants disdain. If someone hates me, again, that's their issue. My role is to be kind and amicable to everyone, even showing detractors their error, not out of spite or to flaunt my patience, but with genuine kindness, like the esteemed Phocion—if he was sincere. That's our internal benchmark, and how the gods should find us: free of bitterness or grievance. After all, what detriment is it to you if you're currently acting in harmony with your nature, and embracing what the universe now finds timely, especially as someone committed to the common good?

14. They scorn each other while attempting to win each other's favor, and they bow to each other while striving to outdo one another.

15. How corrupt and dishonest is the person who declares, "I've decided to be straightforward with you." What are you doing?

There's no need for such an announcement. It should become obvious soon enough; it ought to be visible on your face at first glance. Your voice should convey it instantly, and it should be evident in your eyes—just as lovers instantly recognize everything in each other's gaze. A good and honest person should be like this: when someone is near them, they should feel it immediately, whether they wish to or not. But feigning simplicity is like wielding a dagger. Nothing is more despicable than the friendship of a wolf. Above all, avoid this. The good, the honest, and the kind have these qualities in their eyes, and it doesn't go unnoticed.

16. The ability to live well comes from the soul, if one remains indifferent to things of no consequence. And one will remain indifferent if they consider each thing individually and as a whole, remembering that none of these things forms an opinion about itself within us, nor approaches us, but rather they stay unchanged while we are the ones who form judgments about them and, so to speak, imprint them upon ourselves—though it is within our power not to imprint them and, if they slip by unnoticed, to immediately erase them. Remember, also that this level of attention is only necessary for a short while, after which life will end. Indeed, what is so hard about accepting these things as they are? If they align with nature, take joy in them and find them easy to accept. But if they go against nature, seek what aligns with your own nature, and pursue it, even if it brings no fame. Everyone is excused for seeking their own benefit.

17. Reflect on where each thing originates, what elements each thing is made of, what changes it undergoes, what it becomes after changing, and understand that it suffers no harm.

. . .

18. First, consider what my relationship is to others, and that we were created for each other; and from another perspective, I was created to lead them, just as a ram leads his flock or a bull his herd. Begin with this premise: if not atoms, then a nature that governs the whole. If the latter, then the lesser exist for the sake of the greater, and the greater for the sake of each other.

Second, think about what kind of people they are at the dinner table, in bed, and so forth. Above all, consider the compulsions their opinions subject them to, and how they take pride in those very actions.

Third, if they are acting appropriately, there's no reason to be upset. But if they are acting inappropriately, it's clear they do so unwillingly and out of ignorance. For just as no soul willingly gives up the truth, no soul willingly fails to act rightly toward others. That's why it hurts people to be called unjust, ungrateful, greedy, and in short, harmful to their neighbors.

Fourth, you yourself commit many wrongs and are just like them. And even if you abstain from certain wrongs, you still have the inclination to commit them, even if you avoid similar wrongs due to cowardice, desire for reputation, or some other ignoble reason.

Fifth, you haven't even determined whether they are truly doing wrong, for many actions are part of a larger scheme. And overall, one must learn many things before he can definitively judge another's actions.

Sixth, when you feel overly angry or even despondent, remember that human life is brief, and soon we will all be gone.

Seventh, it's not their actions that disturb us, because those reside in their own minds, but rather our opinions of them. So, discard your opinion, be willing to release your judgment of these actions as terrible, and your anger will disappear. How can you discard your opinion? By realizing that their misdeeds don't harm you. For if wrongdoing were the only evil, you too would be forced into many wrongs, becoming a thief and much worse.

Eighth, consider how much worse the consequences of anger and sorrow are than the events that sparked our anger and sorrow in the first place.

Ninth, kindness is unbeatable, if it's sincere and not a sarcastic smile or an act of deceit. What can the most insolent person do to you if you continue to be kind to him, and, when possible, you gently correct him and calmly point out his mistake at the very moment he tries to harm you, saying, "No, my child, we are meant for something else. I will not be harmed, but you are harming yourself, my child." And show him gently, without any hint of criticism, that this is true, that not even bees behave this way, nor any social animal. But you must do this sincerely and without any bitterness in your heart, not as if lecturing him, and not to be admired by others, but as if he were the only one present, even if others are watching.

Remember these nine lessons from the Muses, and start living as a human being. Guard equally against getting angry with them and pandering to them, for both behaviors are antisocial and lead to harm. And in moments of anger, keep this thought handy: that anger is not manly, but a gentle and kind disposition is more human and therefore more masculine. For to the extent that such a disposition is closer to strength of mind, it is also closer to power. And just as sorrow is a sign of weakness, so is anger. Those who succumb to sorrow and anger have been defeated and have given up.

And if you wish, accept also a tenth lesson from the leader of the Muses: expecting bad people not to commit wrongs is foolish, for that is hoping for the impossible. But to allow them to harm others while insisting they do not harm you is selfish and tyrannical.

. . .

19. Be ever vigilant of these four distortions of your inner guide, and upon recognizing them, clear them away, declaring: "This thought is unnecessary; this thought undermines unity; this is not my true self speaking." For, to speak insincerely is one of the gravest errors. The fourth distortion is self-criticism, which is essentially surrendering the divine within you to the lesser, mortal part—the body and its impulses, whether harsh or gentle.

20. The elements of air and fire within you, inclined to rise, comply with the universe's order and stay grounded within your composite nature. Similarly, the elements of earth and water, inclined to fall, ascend and maintain a stance against their nature. In this way, the elements adhere to the whole, staying in their assigned places until the end signals their release.

Is it not disgraceful, then, that your intellect should be the only part to rebel and resent its role? It faces no coercion, nothing against its nature—yet it defects and moves in the opposite direction. Its inclinations toward injustice, excess, anger, pain, and fear are nothing but a betrayal of nature. And when the intellect resists any situation, it forsakes its duty. It is designed for devotion and respect towards the gods, just as much as for justice. These, too, are expressions of community—and hold even greater honor than mere fairness.

21. "One who lacks a consistent purpose in life cannot maintain consistency throughout life." But identifying the purpose isn't enough—you must also discern its nature. For, just as percep-

tions of "the good" differ among people, it's not universally the same. Instead, the goal must foster community and civic responsibility. Anyone who aligns their motivations with this objective will act consistently, thus remaining the same person throughout.

22. Consider both the mountain mouse and the house mouse; while both may stir, it is the latter that exhibits frantic fear and makes desperate escapes.

23. Socrates described popular opinions as "children's bogeymen"—nothing but illusions and scare tactics.

24. At public events, the Spartans offered their foreign guests seats in the shade, while they themselves sat without special regard for comfort or status.

25. When Perdiccas invited Socrates to his court, Socrates declined, stating: "I refuse, to avoid the worst fate"—implying the burden of receiving favors he could not reciprocate.

26. The Epicureans advised constantly reminding oneself of the ancients who exemplified virtue.

27. The Pythagoreans counseled: Each morning, gaze at the sky to remind yourself of those beings who eternally fulfill their duties following unchanging principles and methods, and to

appreciate their order, purity, and transparency; for no star is hidden.

28. Reflect on Socrates, wearing only his simple cloak after Xanthippe took his robe to wear outside. Consider what Socrates said to his embarrassed friends who hesitated upon seeing him so dressed.

29. In writing and reading, you must follow before you can lead. This principle is even more applicable to life.

30. You are a slave by nature, lacking any portion of reason.

31. But my dear heart laughed within me[3].

32. They will criticize virtue with harsh words[4].

33. Searching for figs in winter is a fool's pursuit. Similarly foolish is the person who seeks their child when it is no longer possible.

34. Epictetus advised that when kissing your child, you should inwardly say: "Perhaps you will die tomorrow." — "Those are ominous words." — "Nothing is ominous," he replied, "if it signifies a natural process. Otherwise, speaking of harvesting grain would also be ominous."

. . .

35. The unripe grape, the ripe grape, the raisin—all undergo transformation, not into nothingness, but into something not yet existing.

36. No one can steal your will (a saying of Epictetus).

37. He stated that one must master the art of agreement, and in the realm of impulses, ensure they are exercised with caution, are community-oriented, and proportional to their value. We should completely avoid desire and not attempt to escape anything beyond our control.

38. The struggle, he said, is not over something insignificant, but about being sane or insane.

39. Socrates used to ask: "What do you desire? The souls of rational or irrational beings?" — "Of rational beings." — "What kind of rational beings? Healthy or corrupt?" — "Healthy." — "Then why don't you seek them out?" — "Because we already possess them." — "Then why do you argue and fight?"

BOOK 12

1. ALL THAT YOU HOPE TO ACHIEVE THROUGH INDIRECT MEANS, YOU can possess now, if you don't deny them to yourself. This means: if you let go of the past, entrust the future to providence, and devote the present entirely to piety and justice. Piety, so you may embrace your destined path, for nature has led you to it and you to nature. Justice, so you may speak truthfully and without deception, and act in accordance with law and the true value of things. Let nothing deter you—not the malice of others, nor public opinion, nor the impulses of the flesh that envelops you. The affected part will manage itself.

Therefore, when you reach the end, cast aside all else and honor only your rational faculty and the divine within you. Do not fear the end of life, but fear never beginning to live according to nature. You will be a man worthy of the universe that created you, no longer a stranger in your own land, no longer bewildered by everyday occurrences as if they were unforeseen, and no longer dependent on anything external.

. . .

2. God perceives all minds as they truly are, free from their physical forms and imperfections; for He engages directly with only those aspects that stem from His own essence. If you train yourself to adopt this perspective, you will free yourself from many distractions. After all, if you pay no mind to the body that surrounds you, how much less will you concern yourself with clothes, housing, reputation, and other superficial trappings?

3. Your existence comprises three components: body, breath, and mind. Of the first two, your role is merely to look after them, but the third—your mind—is truly yours. If you detach from your mind everything that others do or say, everything you have done or said, all that worries you about the future, all that pertains to your body and breath beyond your control, and all that external chaos sweeps in, so that your intellect, freed from fate's snare, can live unburdened, focusing on justice, accepting what happens, and speaking truth—if you rid this governing part of yourself of all attachments to passion, past and future, and emulate Empedocles' sphere, "delighting in its splendid isolation, content in its proper place," committing to live solely in the present, then you can spend the rest of your days until death in serenity, benevolence, and harmony with your guiding spirit.

4. I've often pondered why we each value ourselves so highly, yet hold our own opinions of ourselves in lower regard than those of others. Indeed, if a deity or a wise mentor were to command someone to express every thought or intention in his mind openly, he would find it unbearable even for a day. This clearly shows we hold our neighbors' opinions above our own, caring more about their perceptions than our self-assessment.

· · ·

5. It puzzles me how the gods, having arranged everything so thoughtfully and with benevolence towards humanity, seemingly overlooked that some virtuous individuals, despite their close communion with the divine through sacred rites and sacrifices, should cease to exist after death rather than continue living. However, if this is indeed the case, rest assured it was not overlooked. If it were just, it would have been feasible, and if it were natural, nature would have made it so. The fact that it hasn't happened, assuming it hasn't, should convince you it wasn't necessary. By questioning this, you're essentially debating with the gods; yet, we wouldn't engage in such disputes if they weren't supremely benevolent and just. And if they are, then they wouldn't have allowed any aspect of the universe's design to be neglected or managed unjustly and irrationally.

6. Get used to the things you've left behind. For instance, the left hand, though less adept at many tasks due to lack of practice, holds the reins tighter than the right hand because it's been trained for this specific purpose.

7. Reflect on the state death will find you in, both physically and spiritually: the fleeting nature of life, the vast expanse of time stretching infinitely before and after, and the fragility of all physical matter.

8. Examine things without their superficial layers: the root causes, the purposes behind actions, the essence of pain, pleasure, death, and fame, who is responsible for your dissatisfaction, the realization that no one else can impede your progress, and that all is a matter of perspective.

· · ·

9. In living by your principles, be more like a pancratiast[1] than a gladiator. Unlike the gladiator, who alternates between wielding and discarding his weapon, the pancratiast is always ready, needing only to clench his fist.

10. Approach things by dissecting them into their material, cause, and significance.

11. Consider the power one possesses to do nothing but what God finds acceptable, and to welcome whatever God bestows.

12. It's not just to blame the gods, as they commit no wrong, whether deliberately or accidentally, nor should we blame humans, who act out of ignorance. Thus, blame should be cast upon no one.

13. It's absurd and misplaced to be astonished by any event in life.

14. There are three possibilities: an unchangeable destiny, a benevolent Providence, or chaotic disorder without a guide. If destiny is fixed, resistance is futile. If a kind Providence exists, strive to merit divine assistance. In a world of chaos, take solace in possessing an inner guiding rationale. Even if chaos engulfs you, let it take only your physical being, for it cannot seize your reasoning mind.

. . .

15. Can a lamp's light maintain its glow until extinguished, while the virtues within you—truth, justice, and self-control—falter before your life ends?

16. When you perceive someone has made a mistake, question, "How can I be sure it was indeed a mistake?" Even if it was, understand that the person has already judged themselves, akin to self-inflicted harm.

Expecting the worst of people not to act accordingly is folly, for it wishes for the impossible. To tolerate their harm towards others yet expect immunity for yourself is both unreasonable and oppressive.

17. If it's not just, refrain from doing it; if it's not truthful, refrain from saying it. Control your impulses. Always scrutinize the source of your perceptions, breaking them down into their cause, substance, significance, and the limited time they have to exist.

19. Have you ever felt that there's something within you, greater and more divine than the impulses driving your passions and desires? What dominates my mind now—is it fear, suspicion, desire, or something else?

20. First, act purposefully, never without reason. Second, ensure your guiding principle seeks nothing but the common good.

. . .

21. Soon, you will be gone, as will everything you now see and everyone alive today. Everything in nature is destined to change, transform, and eventually perish, making way for new existences.

22. Perception is everything, and perception lies within your control. Remove, when you wish, your judgments, and like a sailor rounding a cape, you'll find tranquility, stability, and a serene harbor.

23. Every action, when it ends at the right time, experiences no harm for having ended. Likewise, the person who ends these actions, or life itself, at the right moment suffers no harm. The right time is determined by nature, sometimes our own nature, as in old age, but ultimately by the universal nature. Through the transformation of its parts, the universe remains eternally youthful and vibrant. What benefits the whole is always good and timely. Therefore, the end of life is not an evil for the individual, as it is neither shameful - since it is beyond one's control and not detrimental to the community - nor harmful, but rather beneficial and in harmony with the universe. For one is aligned with divine will when moving in the same direction as the divine and sharing its purpose.

24. Keep these three principles at hand. Regarding your actions, ensure they are not impulsive and align with Justice herself. Regarding external events, understand they result from either chance or Providence—blame not chance nor accuse Providence. Reflect on the nature of each thing, from its inception to its end, its composition, and its dissolution. If you could observe

human affairs from above, you would see their insignificance and the vastness of the universe, realizing the folly of pride.

25. Eliminate judgment, and you find liberation. What then prevents you from doing so?

26. When troubled, remember: all occurs according to universal Nature; the fault lies elsewhere; events unfold now as they always have, universally; the bond between humanity and each individual is not of matter but of intellect. Forget not that each person's intellect is divine; nothing truly belongs to us—our children, bodies, and souls all stem from a higher source; perception shapes our reality; only the present is ours to live and to lose.

27. Reflect on those who were once consumed by anger, those who achieved great glory or faced misfortune, enmity, or any twist of fate. Now ask yourself: where has all that gone? To smoke and ashes, to mere tales, or perhaps not even remembered at all. Consider such examples: Fabius Catullinus in his country estate, Lusius Lupus in his gardens, Stertinius at Baiae, Tiberius on Capri, and Velius Rufus—overall, the vanity of seeking to stand out in any way. How futile are all pursuits of distinction, and how much more virtuous it is to be just, self-controlled, and in harmony with the divine, simply adapting to the circumstances life presents. For vanity, even when it pretends to humility, is the most unbearable of all.

· · ·

28. To those questioning, "How can you be sure of the gods' existence or their nature to worship them so devoutly, when you've never seen them?" I say, the gods can indeed be perceived. Moreover, I've never seen my own soul, yet I honor it. Thus, through my constant experience of their influence, I am convinced of the gods' existence and I hold them in reverence.

29. The essence of living well is to see each thing clearly for what it truly is—its substance, its purpose. To act with justice wholeheartedly, and to speak truthfully. What more is there to life than to enjoy it, seamlessly connecting one joy to another, leaving no room for gaps?

30. There is but one sun's light, though it may be blocked by walls, mountains, and numerous other obstacles. There is one universal essence, though it may be divided among countless beings, each with its own characteristics. There is one soul, though it is spread among innumerable forms and individual confines. There is one intellect, though it appears fragmented. The other components, like spirits and physical entities, lack awareness and have no natural connection to each other. Yet, they too are bound by a unifying force and a gravitational pull. The intellect, however, uniquely seeks and merges with what is similar to it, maintaining a sense of community uninterrupted.

31. What do you desire? Merely to continue breathing? To feel, to desire, to grow, then to stop growing, to speak, to think? Which of these do you truly value? If you can easily dismiss each, then consider the ultimate pursuit: to align with reason

and the divine. It's contradictory to value these yet fear death, which merely ends them.

32. Consider how fleeting our share of infinite, unfathomable time is, quickly absorbed into eternity. How minor a portion of the whole essence? How tiny a fragment of the universal soul? How insignificant a speck of the vast earth do we occupy? Reflecting on this, deem nothing important except living according to your true nature and accepting what the universal nature assigns.

33. The key question is how the mind utilizes itself, for everything hinges on this. Everything else, whether within your control or not, is inconsequential, mere dust and shadows.

34. The most compelling reason to not fear death is this: even those who believe pleasure is good and pain is bad have managed to look beyond it.

35. For someone who understands that only the present moment matters, who doesn't care if they perform more or fewer actions guided by sound reasoning, and who is indifferent to whether they observe the universe for a longer or shorter period—such a person does not fear death.

36. Consider yourself a resident of this vast city (the cosmos). What does it matter if you reside here for five years or three? What is just is equal for everyone, according to the laws. So,

what is there to fear if you're not expelled by a tyrant or an unjust judge, but by Nature, the very entity that brought you here? It's like a director who, after hiring an actor, decides to let him go from the stage.

"But I have not performed all five acts, only three."

Your point is valid. However, in life, three acts can constitute the entire play. The completion of the play is decided by the same force that initiated its creation and now calls for its end. You have control over neither. Therefore, leave with a thankful heart, for the entity granting you release is benevolent.

NOTES

Book 1

1. Here the meaning is not a male sibling but rather a male associate.
2. His adoptive father - the Emperor Antoninus Pius.

Book 3

1. The "supreme city" refers to the cosmos or the universe at large, where all humans are citizens.

Book 4

1. Logos
2. One of the Fates.

Book 5

1. This blunt metaphor is meant to highlight the folly of prioritizing material wealth and status over virtue and wisdom.
2. Overdramatizing life's events.
3. Compromising your principles.

Book 6

1. Crates and Xenocrates were ancient Greek philosophers. Crates was known for his ascetic lifestyle and criticism of worldly pursuits, while Xenocrates was a key figure in Plato's Academy.

Book 9

1. The metaphor suggests that children's immature behavior and play-acting are akin to the insubstantial shades of the dead in the Underworld, highlighting the fleeting and trivial nature of such concerns.

Book 11

1. Pancratium/Pankration was an ancient Greek martial art that combined boxing and wrestling.
2. The Cynic philosopher
3. Homer, Odyssey IX, 413
4. Hesiod, Works and Days, 186

Book 12

1. Referring to Pancratium/Pankration - an ancient Greek martial art that combined boxing and wrestling.

www.ingramcontent.com/pod-product-compliance
Lightning Source LLC
Chambersburg PA
CBHW030324160726
47992CB00005B/2154